Le Corbusier

Architect of the Twentieth Century

Text by Kenneth Frampton

Principal Photography by Roberto Schezen

Harry N. Abrams, Inc., Publishers, New York

Commissioning Editor: Diana Murphy
General Editor: Richard Olsen
Copy Editor: David Brown
Designer: Judy Hudson, Biproduct
Production: Alyn Evans

Library of Congress Cataloging-in-Publication Data
Frampton, Kenneth.
Le Corbusier, architect of the twentieth century /
text by Kenneth Frampton ; principal photography
by Roberto Schezen.
    p. cm.
Includes index.
ISBN 0–8109–3494–9
1. Le Corbusier, 1887–1965—Criticism and interpre-
tation. I. Title: Le Corbusier. II. Title: Architect of the
twentieth century. III. Schezen, Roberto.
IV. Title.
NA1053.J4 F693 2002
720'.92—dc21   2002002252

Harry N. Abrams, Inc.
100 Fifth Avenue
New York, N.Y. 10011
www.abramsbooks.com

Abrams is a subsidiary of

LA MARTINIÈRE
G R O U P E

Note to the reader:
The colors chosen for this monograph were
selected from Le Corbusier's Claviers de couleurs
(1931) and Salubra Collection (1959).

Contents

Introduction

Kenneth Frampton

As I have written elsewhere, we shall never finish with Le Corbusier. His output was so prodigious that no single scholar has been able to master all the ramifications of his protean creativity. He was not only the "Architect of the Century," as the British Arts Council characterized him in 1987, on the occasion of an exhibition commemorating the centennial of his birth, but he was also the inventor of a powerful syntax that in one way or another would influence the work of countless architects. Le Corbusier (1887–1965) bequeathed to the world a structurally rigorous but spatially flexible method that no other pioneer of the modern movement would equal. Not even Frank Lloyd Wright, with his romantically expansive vision, could engender anything like the fertility of the Corbusian *parti pris*. For what the Franco-Swiss master proffered was a series of spatial types that possessed a capacity for future development that he himself would never fully exhaust.

Two closely related, canonical paradigms informed his architectonic vision of the early 1920s. The first was his "Dom-Ino" system, derived from François Hennebique's 1892 perfection of the reinforced concrete frame, which Le Corbusier reinterpreted as a double-square with flat slab cantilevers extending front and back beyond the line of the frame. The second, the free plan, *le plan libre,* was finally perfected in the Maison Cook of 1926 in Boulogne-sur-Seine, France. The concept turned on the independence of non-load-bearing partitions from the points of the structural support. The Maison Cook also gave material form to the Purist vision of a new way of life; at the top of the house a library-cum-roof garden overlooked a sea of trees. This was the elevation of the "new man" to a belvedere under the stars. It is a vision that he would return to repeatedly in his early career – an urbane synthesis of a café terrace with the deck of an ocean liner. This was a dandified, bourgeois view of the world but radically new nonetheless, an elite personification of the spirit of modernity precisely captured elsewhere, at the same time, in the photographs of Jacques-Henri Lartigue.

All of this will attain its most condensed, intellectual expression in the Purist school of painting that he and his urbane colleague Amedeé Ozenfant founded out of their mutual critique of both Cubism and Futurism – their *Aprés le Cubisme,* to cite the title of the manifesto that accompanied the first exhibition of their joint Purist works in 1918. Surely no early work by Le Corbusier encapsulates more succinctly the iconic ethos of Purism than his 1920 painting *Nature morte a la pile d'assiettes.* As this abstract "picture-type" reveals, Purism was as much an ideological celebration of industrial civilization, exhibiting the "ready-made" lexicon of everyday life, as it was an aesthetic discourse conceived as an end in and of itself. Abstracted from the bohemian life of the Parisian metropolis, the familiar Cubist icons are posited here as a new form of decorative art: a guitar, a pile of plates, clay pipes (interlocking about the neck of a glass), the ambiguous image of a petrified open book that might just as well be an architectural molding, plus two bottles projected simultaneously in both plan and section.

C.E. Jeanneret (Le Corbusier). *Nature morte a la pile d'assiettes.* 1920

These *objets trouvés,* symbolic of a liberated, metropolitan life, were augmented in Le Corbusier's environmental vision of the early 1920s by *objets types.* Everyday furnishings and equipment, such as the bentwood chairs of Michel Thonet, British upholstered club armchairs, American office furniture, exposed cast-iron radiators and sanitary ware, mass-produced glass and ceramics, luxury leather goods, gloves, spats, and even Auguste Perret's straw hat, are all iconic facets of Le Corbusier's Purist world, as it came to be assembled in his anti–Art Deco manifesto of 1925, *L'Art decorative d'aujourd'hui.*

Le Corbusier inherited his critical stance from the Viennese iconoclast Adolf Loos, whose 1908 essay "Ornament and Crime" countered the effete aestheticism of Jugendstil applied art with the slogan "the true style of our time already exists." Thus, the architect's Purist worldview embraced a "poetry of equipment" that would be used to represent the missing human presence in the photographic representations of his early houses such as the Villa Stein de Monzie (1926) and Villa Savoye (1928), both of which were envisaged as the ideal *mise-en-scène* of a universal culture of which Le Corbusier and Ozenfant were quite explicit when they wrote in somewhat classicizing terms that:

Primary forms and colors have standard properties (universal properties which permit the creation of a transmittable plastic language). But the utilization of primary forms does not suffice to place the

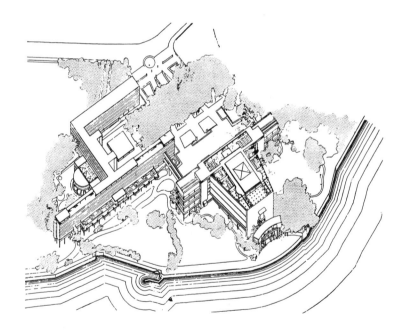

Le Corbusier and Pierre Jeanneret. Project for the League of Nations building, Geneva, Switzerland. 1927. Axonometric

spectator in the sought-for state of mathematical order. For that one must bring to bear the associations of natural or artificial forms, and the criterion for their choice is the degree of selection at which certain elements have arrived (natural selection and mechanical selection). The Purist element issued from the purification of standard forms is not a copy, but a creation whose end is to materialize the object in all its generality and its invariability. Purist elements are thus comparable to words of carefully defined meaning; Purist syntax is the application of the laws which control pictorial space. A painting is a whole (unity); a painting is an artificial formation which, by appropriate means, should lead to the objectification of an entire "world." One could make an art of allusions, an art of fashion, based upon surprise and the conventions of the initiated. Purism strives for an art free of conventions which will utilize plastic constants and address itself above all to the universal properties of the senses and the mind. [1]

No one will ever be able to account fully for what brought about the sudden abandonment of his Purist project at the end of the 1920s. The transformation was anticipated perhaps in the more figurative character that his painting assumed after 1926. One reaches for causal explanations of every conceivable kind. Was the shift precipi-

tated by the denouement of the League of Nations competition of 1927, in which he and his architect–cousin Pierre Jeanneret made a brilliant attempt to render the Purist paradigm at a civic scale? Could it have been the split from Ozenfant and with it the cessation of their magazine *L'Esprit Nouveau?* Or should we account for it by virtue of his revelatory visit to Brazil in 1929 or by the immediate impact of the Great Crash or the difficulties he encountered in the Soviet Union as he began to build his bureaucratic ministry, the Centrosoyuz, to designs that had been finalized in that year?

Whatever the motivation, the trajectory of his career would take an entirely different course after 1929. The free plan comes to play a more muted role and seems to be almost entirely relinquished in his high-rise structures of the 1930s. At the same time, on the domestic front we witness a return to the vernacular, elaborated in rubble stone and undressed lumber, in his Maison Errazuris projected for Chile in 1930. Meanwhile, he and Pierre Jeanneret abandoned monolithic reinforced concrete construction in favor of the steel frame, as in their four canonical curtain-walled buildings, completed between 1930 and 1933: the Pavillon Suisse, the Cité de Refuge, and the Immeuble Porte Molitor apartments, all in Paris, and his equally "machinist" Immeuble Clarté realized in Geneva in 1933.

2561

Le Corbusier and Pierre Jeanneret.
Maison Errazuris, Chile. 1930.
Perspective of interior

Le Corbusier and Pierre Jeanneret.
Apartment building near the Porte
Molitor, Paris, France. 1933.
Perspective of street-facing facade

B 2869

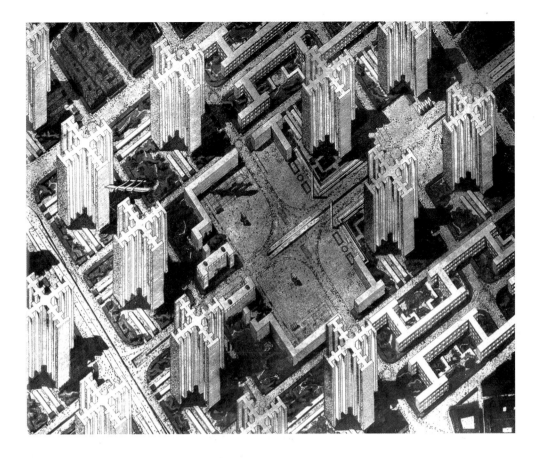

Le Corbusier and Pierre Jeanneret.
Plan Voisin for Paris, France. 1922–25.
Axonometric

At the very moment that Le Corbusier and Pierre Jeanneret embraced rationalized dry assembly and endorsed, in principle, fully air-conditioned structures – a technique that was hopelessly in advance of its time in Europe – they simultaneously turned to an intermediate technology in their post-Purist, domestic work. Archaic techniques, especially load-bearing, rubble-stone walls, find themselves combined, as in the canonical Maison Week-end of 1934, with industrialized building techniques ranging from glass lenses and steel-framed plate glass picture windows to shell concrete vaults, machine-made ceramic tiles, and sheet plywood linings. The shell concrete vault, first broached in his Maison Monol, projected in 1919, now reappears in a modified form and in a totally different context. It will persist as a key domestic trope throughout the remainder of his career, from his Peyrissac House, projected for Cherchell, North Africa, in 1942, to the Maisons Jaoul built in Neuilly-sur-Seine, near Paris, in 1955, and the Villa Sarabhai realized in Ahmedabad, India, in 1955.

We have ignored until now, given the nature of this anthology, the comprehensive reach of his urban imagination, beginning with his megalomaniacal proposal for a city of three million inhabitants, the *Ville Contemporaine,* first exhibited at the Salon d'Automne in 1922. Three generic type-forms were envisaged as making up the fabric of this ideal city, predicated at a large scale on a double-square and on the antique cosmological cruciform formation of the Roman *cardo* and *decumanus*. These types were: the "Cartesian skyscraper" (his self-conscious antithesis of the American paradigm), cruciform in plan, rising to some sixty stories, and posited as a new generic metropolitan office structure; the residential *bloc à redent,* twelve stories high and based on the zigzag formation of Eugene Henard's *boulevard à redan*s of 1910; and a standard perimeter block rising to the same height as an alternative residential format. Both metropolitan housing types were conceived as having a "palatial" potential whereby, as in Charles Fourier's utopian socialist concept of the *phalanstery*, ordinary citizens would be able to live in a collective dwelling at a monumental scale – as Fourier put it, on the same scale of grandeur as Louis XIV in Versailles. This dense metropolitan "green city" layout will be gradually opened up as an urban model over the next decade until in 1935 it is finally abandoned in favor of freestanding slab blocks organically arranged in loose chevron formation in the midst of continuous parkland.

The year 1935 would prove to be a watershed in this regard, since it is in this year, just after the reformulation of his ideal urban thesis (with his book *La Ville Radieuse*), that he will finally abandon the centralized city model in favor of the linear city, a concept taken as a dynamic urban model from the writings of the Soviet urbanist

N. A. Miliutin, whose book *Sotzgorod* (*Socialist Towns*) had been published in 1930. From now on, as far as urban planning is concerned, he will think in terms of regional urbanization rather than perpetuate hypothetical recapitulations of the old Humanist civic model. However, the decade that separates this moment from the austere but socially progressive era that emerged in Europe after the end of World War II is one in which Le Corbusier goes to ground, as it were, as this is anticipated in his Pavillon des Temps Nouveaux, erected in 1936 for the Paris World Exhibition of 1937. This large canvas tent, suspended from wire cables and braced by lattice girders in steel, was once again a combination of archaic and modern technology. Based on an archaeological reconstruction of the Hebrew Temple in the Wilderness, as this had appeared in Le Corbusier's 1923 manifesto *Vers une architecture,* the Pavillon des Temps Nouveaux is loaded with spiritual if not ecclesiastical connotations, from the acoustical shell rising above the speaker's rostrum like a baldachin, to a sculptural representation of the CIAM (Congrès Internationaux d'Architecture Moderne) Athens Charter of 1934, as though, like the mosaic tablets, this charter was the physical manifestation of a universal ethic. These spiritual evocations were reinforced by the Popular Front slogan inscribed on the inside of the acoustic shell: "a new era has begun, an era of solidarity."

It is virtually this same ethos that will prompt the development of the Unité d'Habitation Marseilles after the war, a project commissioned by the then minister of reconstruction, Raoul Dautry. Le Corbusier's lifelong "utopian socialist" beliefs were to reach their apotheosis in this breathtaking structure, poised on Egyptoid *pilotis* and housing more than three hundred duplex and simplex units of twenty-three different types, from bachelor cells to large family

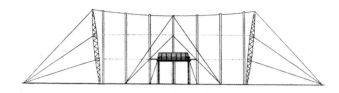

Le Corbusier and Pierre Jeanneret. Pavillion des Temps Nouveaux, Paris, France. 1937. Section

dwellings. The fact that a full range of services was incorporated into this collective dwelling, from rooftop athletic facilities to a shopping street and a small hotel situated halfway up the block, links this heroic apartment building to the pre-Stalinist *dom kommuna* ideals of the Soviet Union in its idealistic prime. While Le Corbusier's socialism was certainly more cultural than political, it nonetheless remained as an implicit value throughout his career. As he put it in the last chapter of *Vers une architecture,* "the various classes of workers in society today no longer have dwellings adapted to their needs; neither the artisan nor the intellectual. It is a question of building which is at the root of the social unrest today; architecture or revolution."

Monolithic reinforced concrete construction, cast in situ, reemerges after the war as the *lingua franca* of his architecture. Now, however, and with the exception of the Millowners' Association Building in Ahmedabad and the Carpenter Center for Visual Arts at Harvard University, we are removed from the free plan, which had been the essential spatial matrix of his Purist period. The spatial dynamism of his architecture is still palpably in evidence, but it no longer depends on a displacement between the volumetric subdivision and the points of support. The *pilotis* play a more limited role in this period as the walls are brought straight down to the ground to assume a new importance. At the same time, concrete cast from rough wooden formwork, the *"bêton brut,"* imparts a phenomenological intensity to the overall form wherein buildings such as the monastery of La Tourette in Eveux-sur-l'Arbresle seem to rise out of the ground like the force of a telluric demiurge – tragic and timeless in character almost by definition. Even though he increasingly embraces the principles of a wall architecture, Le Corbusier's work is just as typological as it was before – perhaps even more so in terms of its hybrid character. In this regard La Tourette is an amalgam of Mount Athos and the Charterhouse of Ema in Tuscany, both monastic models having impressed him in his youth, while the Millowners' Association Building, the Villa Shodan in Ahmedabad (1954), and the Carpenter Center for the Visual Arts are all to be seen as reworkings of his

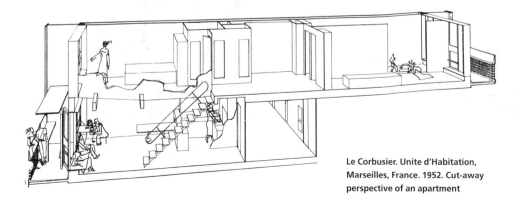

Le Corbusier. Unite d'Habitation, Marseilles, France. 1952. Cut-away perspective of an apartment

Neo-Palladian, *palazetto* format, which had first manifested itself in the Villa Stein de Monzie in Vaucresson, France, in 1926.

It can be shown that Le Corbusier's typological-cum-metaphorical habit of mind applies even to an ecclesiastical form as unorthodox as the Chapel of Nôtre Dame-du-Haut built at Ronchamp in 1955. Here a peculiarly dense fusion is achieved between a number of different types; grounded, in the first instance, in the white vernacular of the Mediterranean but going on to combine in its astonishingly complex form sources as varied as the Acropolis, subterranean Bronze Age crypts in Malta, the Hebrew Temple in the Wilderness (via the Pavillon des Temps Nouveaux), and even something as innocent as a crab shell found on a Long Island beach.

Le Corbusier's Indian work of the mid-1950s returns us to the dichotomous house/palace theme that had first been elaborated on in his essay *"Une maison – un palais"* of 1928. In it he argued, in a somewhat oracular manner, that a palace, that is, a symmetrical Neo-Palladian type-form, may be given all the empirical convenience of a modern dwelling through the functional capacity of the free plan whereas an organically planned house may be accorded the dignity of a palace through the rigorous application of harmonic proportions, by which he meant, at a later date, through the use of his *Modulor* system of proportion, which, first published in 1950, was based on the time-honored principle of the square versus the Golden Section rectangle – the universal proportion of 1:1.618. Thus, he sets up a series of interrelated conceptual oppositions: palace versus house, formal versus empirical, classic versus romantic. We are here confronted with that dualistic mode of beholding that would serve as his primary *modus operandi* throughout his life.

Hence, the Apollo versus the Medusa, the one calm and smiling, the other disconsolate and raging, a schism with which he appears to identify himself after 1942 when the icon first appears at the end of his book *La Maison des Hommes.* This image condenses better than any other artifact the essentially dialogical character of his thought from the early 1920s onward. Here the tragic darkness of the irrational is set against the shining light of Olympian reason just as, at an entirely different level in *La Maison des Hommes,* the figure of the architect comes to be dialectically opposed to that of the engineer. In all these conjunctions the two halves of the dichotomy are patently inseparable; they constitute a fertilizing dualism wherein the one depends upon the other. As he put it in *Vers une architecture:*

The Engineer's Aesthetic and Architecture – two things that march together and follow one from the other – the one at its full height, the other in an unhappy state of retrogression.
The Engineer, inspired by the law of Economy and governed by mathematical calculation, puts us in accord with universal law. He achieves harmony.
The Architect, by his arrangement of forms, realizes an order which is a pure creation of his spirit; by forms and shapes he affects our senses to an acute degree, and provokes plastic emotions; by the relationships which he creates he wakes in us profound echoes, he gives us the measure of an order which we feel to be in accordance with that of our world, he determines the various movements of our heart and of our understanding; it is then that we experience the sense of beauty.[2]

Le Corbusier was painter and architect at the same time; a comparable polarity determined the oscillation of his working life on a daily basis. From 1924 to 1952 he devoted the mornings to painting and writing and the afternoons to architecture while from 1953 until his death in 1965 this alternation was reversed. A more interpersonal duality also effected the most fertile collaborations of his creative life. The intellectual and painterly interests linking him to Amedeé Ozenfant over the period of Purism (1917 to 1925) is paralleled, in the professional architectural domain, by the bond tying him to his architect–cousin Pierre Jeanneret, who during the course of their partnership (1923 to 1940) played an indispensable role in the practical realization of the works of the office. That

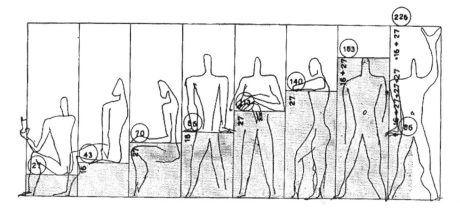

Le Corbusier. Le Modulor System. 1950

such a role, however essential, was at odds with Le Corbusier's quixotic temperament is born out by Le Corbusier's later characterization of their relationship as: "I am the sea and he is the mountain and as everyone knows these two can never meet."[3]

As to the influence that this turbulent-creativity had on the course of twentieth-century architecture as a whole, I shall confine myself here to citing only some of those who, across the best part of the century, were quite obviously influenced by him in terms of both typological method and syntactic form. First and foremost among these were some members of the Russian architectural avant-garde of the 1920s and 1930s who also partially influenced him. I have in mind Mosei Ginzburg, whose 1924 manifesto *Style and Epoch* was a direct response to the thesis of *Vers une architecture* since the main body of Le Corbusier's text had already been published in the pages of *L'Esprit Nouveau*. Ginzburg would follow this riposte with his Narkomfin collective dwelling, realized in Moscow over the years 1928 to 1929, which clearly displays the influence of Le Corbusier's Five Points of a New Architecture: *le plan libre, la facade libre, le toit jardin, le pilotis,* and *le fenêtre en longeur.* A similar line of syntactic influence surely is present in the work of the Russian émigré Berthold Lubetkin, whose Highpoint One apartment block realized in Highgate, London, in 1935, owed much to Le Corbusier, particularly in terms of its liberal use of *pilotis* at grade, along with its freely planned ground floor. In a similar manner, long before

12

Le Corbusier. The Five Points of a New Architecture. 1926

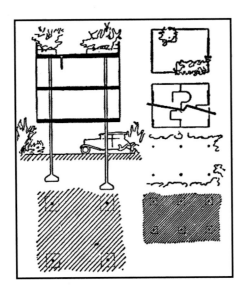

the advent of jet travel and instant telecommunications, his influence would spread across entire continents virtually overnight, from the realization of the Neo-Corbusian National Ministry of Education in Rio de Janeiro, Brazil, to the designs of Oscar Niemeyer, Lucio Costa, and Alfonso Reidy, over the years 1936 to 1943, to the work of Rex Martiensen's so-called Transvaal Group in South Africa, and the architecture of Jaromir Krejcar in Czechoslovakia.

At mid-century, particularly in the years immediately after World War II, the Corbusian influence is present in the Royal Festival Hall, London (1951), designed by Leslie Martin, Peter Moro, and Robert Mathew, and in Alison and Peter Smithson's Golden Lane proposals of 1952, which were inspired by Le Corbusier's Unité d'Habitation, realized in Marseilles in the same year. A decade later, following Le Corbusier's low-rise, high-density housing project, Roq et Rob, designed for Roquebrune-Cap-Martin in 1949, we again discern his influence in Atelier 5's Siedlung Halen housing settlement, realized outside Bern in 1960. By now we have entered an era in which the different paradigms coming from the prewar and postwar phases of his career mutually influence architects in different countries in countervailing ways. Thus, Michael Graves's Hanselman House, projected for Fort Wayne, Indiana, in 1967, is a reinterpretation of Le Corbusier's Purist architecture. The same may still be said twenty years later of José Oubrerie's 1988 French Cultural Centre in Damascus or even of Henri Ciriani's proposal for an archaeological museum in Arles dating from 1991. And yet, more than a decade earlier, in 1977, we find the Japanese architect Tadao Ando picking up where Atelier 5 left off nearly twenty years before in his own *bêton brut* version of low-rise, high-density housing: his Rokko Housing built near Kobe in 1981. On the other hand, more than ten years later in 1993 we encounter Rem Koolhaas's Kunsthal in Rotterdam, which is surely indebted to Le Corbusier's competition project of 1964 for a congress hall in Strasbourg, just as the monumental canopy of Jean Nouvel's concert hall, built in Lucerne in 1999, owes something, however remotely, to the portico of Le Corbusier's assembly building in the Capital of the Punjab in Chandigarh.

And so it goes on with the "Architect of the Century," whose influence ricochets back and forth across the unfolding trajectory of the "new" with which, despite the deliquescence of Postmodernism, we still remain engaged.

Selected Buildings

Villas La Roche-Jeanneret

Paris, 1923–25

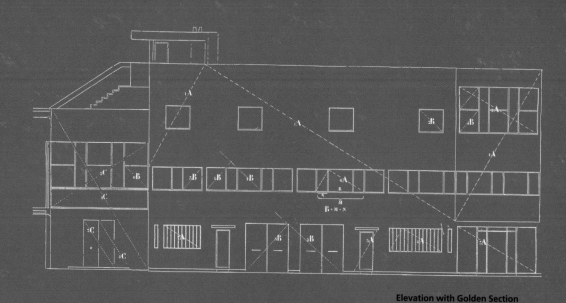

Elevation with Golden Section regulating lines

In 1922 the young lawyer and art collector Raoul La Roche commissioned Le Corbusier and Pierre Jeanneret to design a complex of houses that would flank both sides of a Parisian cul-de-sac. However, La Roche was not able to acquire a site of adequate width, and the complex was reduced to a single long, three-story building accommodating two residences. Even in its truncated form, the scheme was a synthetic expression of Le Corbusier's ideals at the moment when he was elaborating the main principles of his Purist architecture. The attached houses occupy one side of the cul-de-sac while a two-story pavilion, raised on *pilotis* and connected to the larger of the dwellings, juts out at the end of the street. These houses, divided by a party wall, belonged to Le Corbusier's brother, Albert Jeanneret, and to La Roche himself. La Roche's art gallery, elevated on *pilotis,* served as a focal point at the end of the street. Although the two dwellings were linked visually by identical strip windows that made them appear to be a single structure, they differed markedly in both size and plan.

La Roche's villa was the more monumental of the two. A triple-height entry hall allowed visitors to access spaces opening off to the left and right. This volume and the curved ramp-wall in the gallery were the most dramatic spaces of the house.

As one enters the La Roche residence, two voids are cut out of the surface to the left of the entrance. The first of these is a recessed door leading to a ground-floor guest room while the second is a dogleg stair that flows out of the foyer and rises up to assume an abstract, sculptural form. The visitor also is made immediately aware of a seemingly inaccessible, partially top-lit space on the third floor. A similar spatial play is repeated on the entry foyer's right wall, where two service galleries appear open at the second and third floors. Higher-than-usual pipe railings modulate the proportions of these galleries while at the same time providing spatial slots overlooking the triple-height space.

This stair at the left is the main *promenade architecturale* of the house (or spatial journey through it). A small balcony juts out from the top of the stair into the volume of the foyer, interrupting the openness of the space. The stair landing leads to the double-height gallery that curves out towards the cul-de-sac. The first-floor landing opens onto a *passarelle* that bridges over the entrance hall and into the dining room. This is served in turn by a smaller service stair connecting to the kitchen and the cook's quarters below; it also provides access to a roof garden above. A small terrace next to the dining room admits southern light into the house.

If one continues straight ahead from the stair landing, rather than crossing the *passarelle,* one enters the gallery. A square window to the left of the gallery entrance affords a view up the cul-de-sac. As the wall continues from this window it curves gently outwards, forming the interior of the bulge seen from the street. At the far end of this wall, where a glass door gives access to a small balcony, a ramp rises upwards to give access to the library.

The Villas La Roche-Jeanneret embody what Le Corbusier would later term the first of his Four Compositions, of which he wrote in 1929: "The inside takes its ease and pushes out to form diverse projections." The allusion here is to the traditional Anglo-Saxon Arts and Crafts L-shaped plan to which he would remain attached throughout his life, because of the convenience it afforded, as opposed to the spatial formality of the typical classical villa. However, as he noted, this is a solution that can become fussy and out of control if one isn't careful. Against this he posits his so-called second composition, that is to say, the ideal of the pure prism derived from European classicism. The villas are also the first of his "cubic compositions," a paradigm that, as he pointed out, is satisfying to the intellect but extremely difficult to achieve. He eventually would respond to this challenge by exploiting his concept of the free plan, *le plan libre,* in two alternatives that comprise his third and fourth compositions, the Villa Stein de Monzie of 1926 and the Villa Savoye of 1928.

1.17

Today the Villas La Roche-Jeanneret house the Foundation Le Corbusier, which the architect set up before his death in 1965 to ensure access to his archives and library. The gallery, once furnished with Raoul La Roche's collection, is now hung with works by the architect–artist.

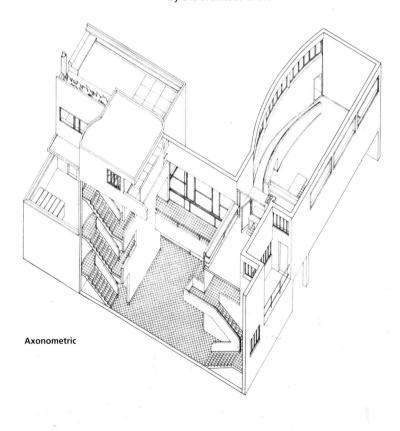

Axonometric

1.19

Early sketch of entry hall. 1923

Various views of entry hall
as it is today

Third-floor mezzanine study with
Le Corbusier, Pierre Jeanneret,
and Charlotte Perriand's chaise
longue of 1929

Dining room

Interior views of double-height
art gallery with ramp to mezzanine
and study

La Petite Maison

Corseaux, Switzerland, 1923–24

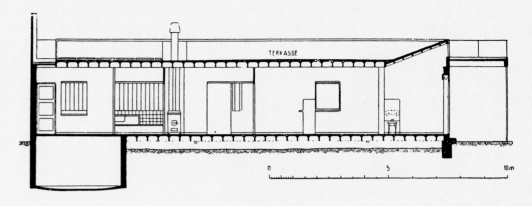

TERRASSE

2.27

Other than the one-room Le Petit Cabanon that he built for himself at Roquebrune-Cap-Martin in his sixty-fifth year, this small house (also known as Villa "Le Lac"), designed for his parents when he was thirty-six, is Le Corbusier's most modest domestic work. It comprises a single-story rectangle sitting on a narrow strip of land on the shore of Lake Geneva. Le Corbusier and Pierre Jeanneret's design for the house seems to have preceded the identification of the site; when they found it, Le Corbusier recalled, it "fit like a glove." As architectural historian Deborah Gans has put it, the "plan contained the idea of a dwelling that could fully express itself only in relation to its desired landscape."

Closed along the shoreline road, which serves as the northern boundary of the property, and almost equally opaque on its narrow ends, the one-room living volume that comprises most of the house is lit exclusively by a horizontal window facing out over the lake. This thirty-six-foot-long opening is the defining element of the house. A guest room at the eastern end of the dwelling is separated from the living space by a sliding–folding screen. The western end is occupied by a kitchen, laundry room, and dressing/bathing space, while a double-bed sleeping alcove opens off the main living area.

A stair running along the short western wall provides access to a roof terrace that extends almost the full length of the house and faces out over the lake. A very small attic study was later added at the top of this stair, adjacent to a double-height, partially latticed wall

Perspective sketch of the site

that shields both the house and its narrow lakefront terrace from the low-angle western sun. The main terrace of the house, protected from the rock scree at the edge of the lake by a low rubble-stone wall, expands at its eastern end to embrace the full width of the site. At this point it also is enclosed on three sides by medium-height stone walls that in effect create a small courtyard garden.

While the abstract style of this house epitomizes the Purist ideal of a machine-age architecture, it alludes simultaneously to the whitewashed vernacular of the Mediterranean. Thus, while the rubble-stone walls are plastered smooth on the lake front, they are simply whitewashed on their inner courtyard faces within the garden patio. Le Corbusier indulges in a play of scale that creates the illusion, particularly from a middle distance, that the patio is larger than its actual dimensions. This effect is produced by the precise

proportions of the stone-framed opening to the lake, capped by a concrete slab and brought down to an extremely low, diminutive concrete table beneath which one can barely put one's knees. An ironic version of this scalar play is introduced into the northeastern corner of the courtyard, where a small grilled aperture lets the resident dog announce his presence to passersby.

Le Corbusier designed La Petite Maison, as he later called it, shortly before his father's death. After his passing, the house continued to serve the family. "His mother spent time there throughout her life," notes Gans, "as did his brother, a composer who used it as a studio. Many photographs survive of family gatherings in the garden. The house still contains personal artifacts such as Mediterranean pottery and an elaborate wooden desk designed by the architect early in his career."

2.28

Early sketch of dining space. 1923

Attic bedroom

Alcove bed space off the living room

Villa Stein de Monzie

Vaucresson, France, 1926–28

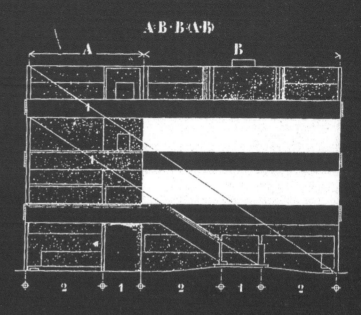

Garden elevation with Golden
Section regulating lines

3.33

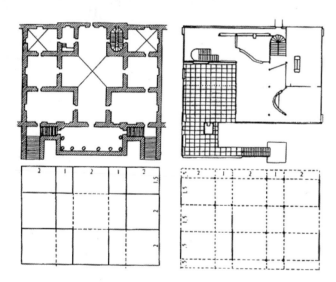

Comparative analysis of the
plans of Palladio's Villa Foscari
(La Malcontenta) of 1559 and
the Villa Stein de Monzie showing comparable proportional
relationships

This house in the suburban town of Garches (now Vaucresson) is
the result of an interesting double commission. The initial client was
Gabrielle de Monzie, the former wife of Anatole de Monzie, who,
as France's minister of construction, had been the patron of Le
Corbusier's Pavillon de l'Esprit Nouveau erected in 1924 for the 1925
Exposition des Arts Décoratifs. The other clients were Michael Stein,
brother of the American writer Gertrude, and his wife, Sarah,
who was a painter and an early collector of Henri Matisse. Gabrielle
de Monzie and the Steins had spent several summers together in
the Steins' Italian Renaissance villa, and, as a result, they asked
Le Corbusier for the modern equivalent of this classical dwelling.

This explicit commission stimulated Le Corbusier's latent Palladianism,
a quality that critic Colin Rowe detailed in his 1948 comparison of
the villa's plan with that of Andrea Palladio's mid-sixteenth-century
Villa Foscari. As Rowe noted, both houses were organized structurally
and conceptually according to the Palladian *a-b-a-b-a* rhythm. In
Le Corbusier's villa, this rhythm was translated into the proportions
2:1:2:1:2. While Palladio made the central portion of his composition dominant, in the Villa Stein de Monzie, as Rowe remarks, "the
central focus has been consistently broken up, concentration at
one point is disintegrated and replaced by a peripheral dispersion of
incident. The dismembered fragments of the central focus become,
in fact, a sort of serial installation of interest round the extremities
of the plan."[4]

Various early sketches. 1926

The Villa Stein de Monzie also departs radically from the Palladian paradigm through the application of two Purist devices: first, Le Corbusier's Five Points of a New Architecture; and second, his particular application of the time-honored Golden Section proportion (1:1.618) in the form of regulating lines superimposed on its front and back facades. These two devices – spatially dynamic yet at the same time controlled – override any trace of historicism. The Villa Stein de Monzie ultimately employed only four of the Five Points: the free plan (*le plan libre*), the free facade (*la facade libre*), the long window (*le fenêtre en longeur*), and the roof garden (*le toit jardin*). The fifth, the Purist *pilotis* that were by now practically a signature element in Le Corbusier's architecture, was suppressed in favor of a more monumental prismatic form, enabling the cantilevered, "stressed skin" front facade to descend to the ground without interruption. However, an atypical single *piloti* does appear at the rear, supporting a cantilevered terrace overlooking the garden.

Although the overall impression of the villa is symmetrical, largely due to its central, roof-level oculus, the organization of the interior is asymmetrical, displaced by rotating the main stair through ninety degrees at the entry level. This single gesture initiates an asymmetrical *promenade architecturale* that ricochets throughout the floor above. At the first floor one passes from the main stair through the library, into the living room, and from there to the dining room, which is separated from the living space by a free-standing, parabolic screen. This spatial sequence continues onto the elevated terrace, which is let into the rear of the basic prism as a paved platform. The promenade concludes with a straight stair leading down into the garden.

Of all the buildings of Le Corbusier's Purist period, the Villa Stein de Monzie has suffered the most. After World War II, it was converted into apartments, an intervention that modified its proportions and utterly destroyed the dynamic spatiality of its interior.

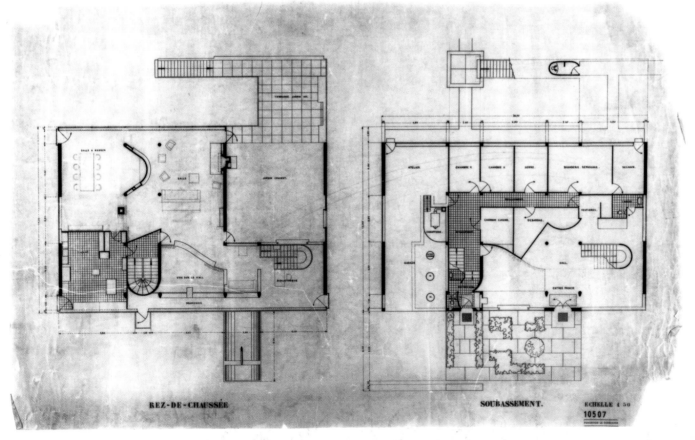

First-floor plan   Second-floor plan

Villa Savoye

Poissy, France, 1928–31

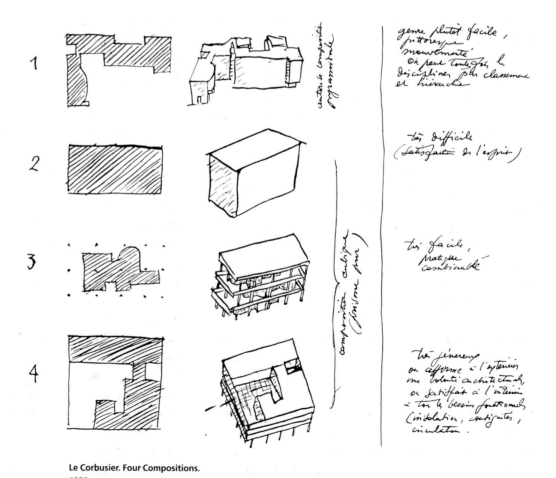

Le Corbusier. Four Compositions.
1929

The Villa Savoye began as a relatively straightforward commission from Pierre and Emilie Savoye, an upper-class Parisian couple who wished to construct a weekend house in the country. Le Corbusier interpreted this modest command on a grand scale and in so doing created one of the key icons of modern European architecture. As the last of Le Corbusier's Purist villas, the Villa Savoye may be seen as the ultimate formulation of the *piloti* concept, an idea that he had first been inspired by as a schoolboy. As architectural historian Adolf Max Vogt informs us, Swiss history textbooks of that era featured illustrations of Paleolithic pile dwellings, the remains of which had recently been discovered on the alpine lakes of Neuchâtel and Bienne. In his maturity Le Corbusier would seem to have inter-jected this prehistoric type into the modern house, thereby pro-ducing the radical vision of a dwelling raised clear of the ground, hovering above a sea of greenery. He first attempted this in his 1925 project for the Villa Meyer and partially realized it the following year in his Maison Cook in Boulogne-sur-Seine on the outskirts of Paris. The idea was only to acquire its full expression in this square, prismatic villa set in a hilltop meadow in Poissy, thirty kilometers (18.6 miles) from Paris.

We know from Le Corbusier's archives that the design of this house was a particularly tortured process. The project went through five different states before a reworked version of the initial sketch was accepted by the clients. The basic strategy of the house was succinctly encapsulated in his *Oeuvre Complete*. "The house must not have a front," Le Corbusier wrote. "Positioned on top of the dome, it must open out to the four horizons. The living floor, with its hanging garden, will be suspended above *piloti* so as to afford distant views over the horizon."[5]

The white, single-story frame of the villa, raised on *pilotis* around its perimeter, does indeed appear to float above the meadow. One's first impression is of the house's exceptional horizontality, with a rib-bon window extending almost the full width of the house, divid-ing its apparently identical facades into three unequal bands. Five *pilotis* on each side provide visible support for the building (there are less visible supports deeper under the structure). An undulating white screen-wall, pierced by a rectangular opening, crowns the house, revealing the presence of a partially concealed roof garden.

That the Villa Savoye was conceived from the outset as a lavish week-end retreat is emphasized by its absolute dependence on automo-tive access. The house is all too clearly organized on the ground floor as an automobile destination, with cars arriving and depart-ing through a *porte cochere* at grade as though they were gondo-las serving the undercroft of a Venetian palazzo. Three cars, one for each member of the Savoye family, can be garaged underneath the house to one side of the main entry. To the left of this garage space is the main entrance of the villa, housed in a quasi-elliptical

transparent box faced with vertical, industrial glazing. One enters through a solid metal door painted black. The well-lit entry hall, with a floor of machine-made ceramic tiles laid on the diagonal, is enlivened by two freestanding sculptural elements: a standard wash-basin and a spiral stair descending from the *piano nobile* above. These two elements, together with the initial rise of the ramp, impart a ritualistic aura to the entrance, inviting one to wash one's hands before ascending to the main body of the house. This side-lit accessway makes a tight switchback turn on its way up. The asymmetrical flow of the ramp as it rises upward leads one into the transverse axis of the living–dining room, which in turn opens out onto an adjacent terrace through a large sliding window-wall facing south. Paved in stone, this elevated terrace gives rise to a further turn of the ramp leading up to the rooftop solarium. This partly cylindrical, partly elliptical sun trap, opening towards the south, is shielded from the north by the undulating screen-wall.

The most labyrinthine space in the house is the top-lit bathroom of the master bedroom suite, where a built-in, tiled *chaise longue* separates the bathing space from the sleeping area. One reaches this point by the spiral stair that affords a more direct means of access between the three levels – the entry (which also contains accommodations for the chauffeur and domestic staff), the *piano nobile,* and the solarium. The *promenade architecturale* that animates the entire complex constantly affords changing views of the bodies circulating in space as they negotiate either the ramp or the stair, the one having glimpses of the other, and vice versa, throughout the height of the building.

As in the Villas La Roche-Jeanneret, the human subject seems to take on a heightened presence in this house as one looks out from the living–dining room to people assembled casually on the terrace or up from the same terrace to a cluster of figures in the solar-

4.42

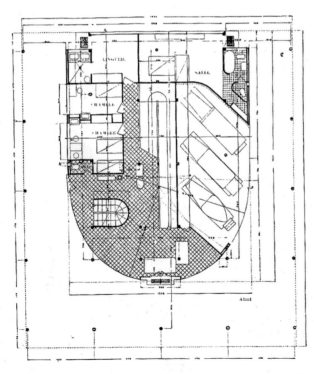

Ground-floor plan

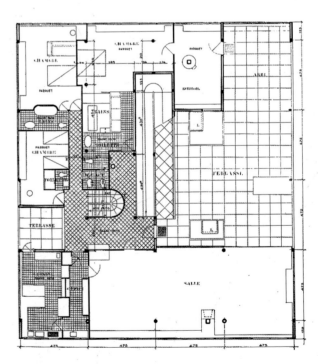

First-floor plan

ium; and from within the ramp, enclosed by horizontal industrial glazing, one gains a glimpse of figures climbing the external ramp to the roof. This sense of continuous spatial movement was reinforced, here as elsewhere in Le Corbusier's work, through subtle displacements in scale such as the exceptionally low table attached to the unglazed, three-bay, horizontal opening framing the first-floor terrace (compare this with the diminutive table overlooking Lake Geneva in La Petite Maison). Further displacements are enforced through the extensive use of color. "Unlike the Villa La Roche," noted Jacques Sbriglio in his book on the villa, "this is never applied in monochrome fashion to all the walls and ceilings of one room." Thus, pink covers one wall of the living room but pale blue coats another; two walls in the Savoyes' son's bedroom are ocher; gray is used on one wall of the master bedroom and a lighter shade on the house's shelving. "The final hues that set off the ensemble," Sbriglio continues, "are the off-white and pale yellow tiles, coupled with the clear oak tones of the strip flooring."[6]

Despite the authority with which Sbriglio describes this color scheme, he is the first to concede that the debate as to how colors originally were deployed will probably never be settled, particularly if we still entertain doubts as to the current colors used on the exterior, with its dark green base capped by an all-white prism. As he notes, the gardener's house is now similarly divided between a white prismatic top and a dark green base even though an archival sketch shows it finished with pale green walls above a dark green base.

As one looks at the crystalline prism of the now-restored Villa Savoye, it is hard to imagine the vicissitudes it has suffered. It began as a leaky, underheated weekend house that the Savoyes endured with mixed feelings for about a decade. The family abandoned the house at the beginning of World War II, and it was soon reduced to a ruin, whereupon it was casually exploited as a hay barn before its total decrepitude inspired an international campaign to save it from demolition. The romantic vistas that it once commanded were long ago compromised by suburban development and by the presence of a nearby school building, although this last has been partially compensated for by a stand of trees that now encloses the meadow and screens the building from the random development to the north. It was finally adopted as a French national monument in the late 1960s under the auspices of André Malraux, who was then the minister of culture.

Early sketch of the first-floor terrace

4.46

Interior of main bathroom on
the first floor

Interior of entry hall with spiral
stair to the first floor

4.50

Interior of ramp leading up to
the first floor

View of external ramp from spiral stair

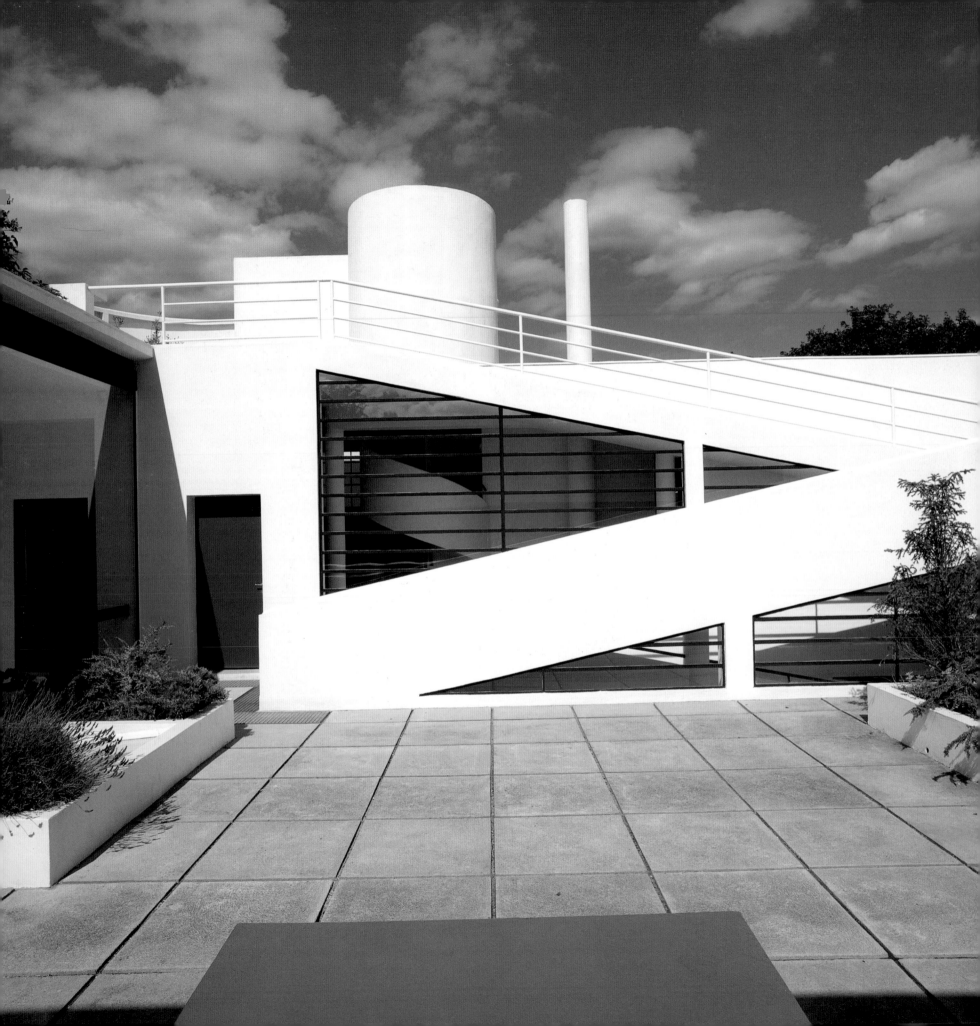

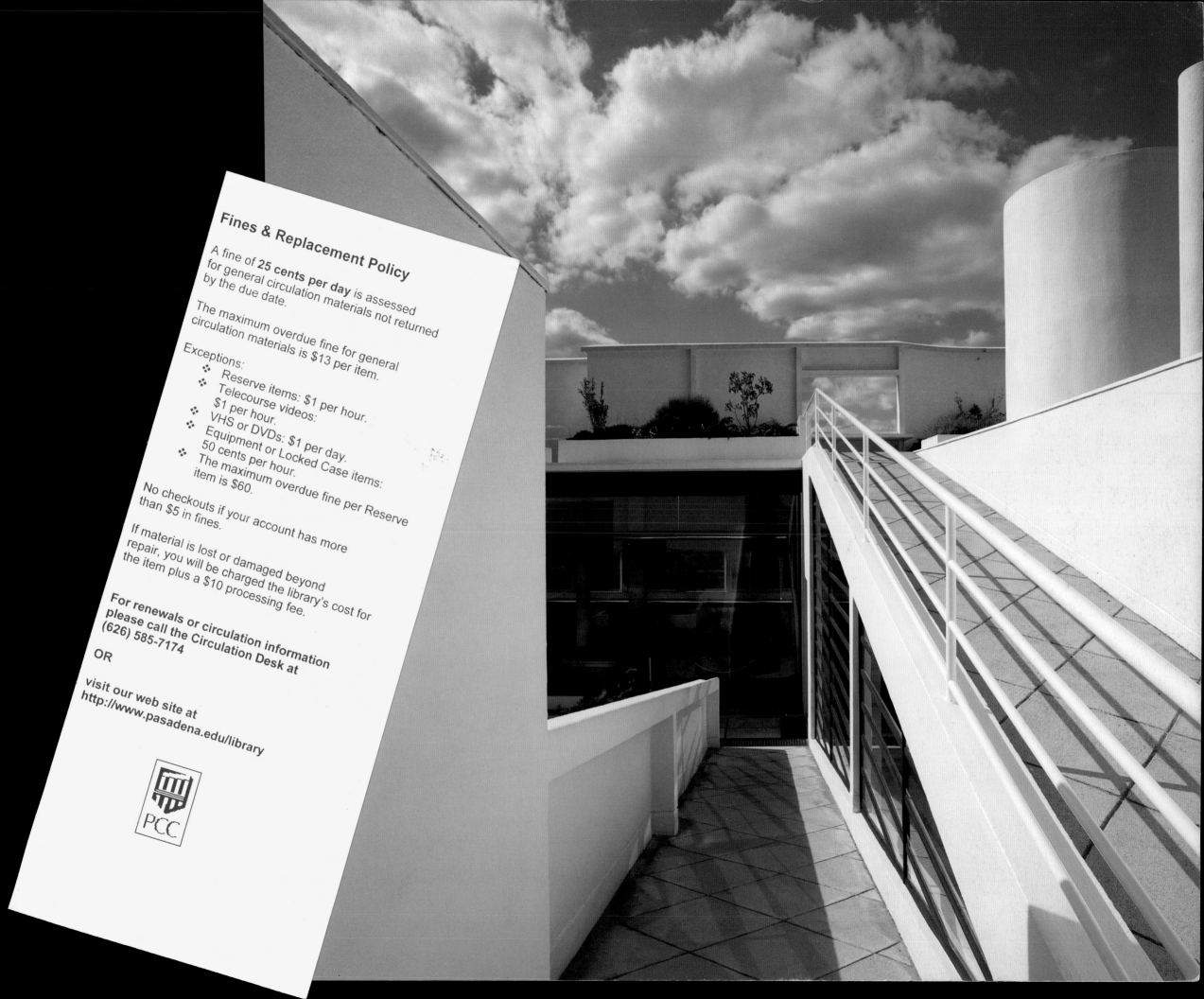

Fines & Replacement Policy

A fine of **25 cents per day** is assessed for general circulation materials not returned by the due date.

The maximum overdue fine for general circulation materials is $13 per item.

Exceptions:
* Reserve items: $1 per hour.
* Telecourse videos: $1 per hour.
* VHS or DVDs: $1 per day.
* Equipment or Locked Case items: 50 cents per hour.
* The maximum overdue fine per Reserve item is $60.

No checkouts if your account has more than $5 in fines.

If material is lost or damaged beyond repair, you will be charged the library's cost for the item plus a $10 processing fee.

For renewals or circulation information please call the Circulation Desk at (626) 585-7174

OR

visit our web site at http://www.pasadena.edu/library

PCC

Cité de Refuge

Paris, 1929–33

&

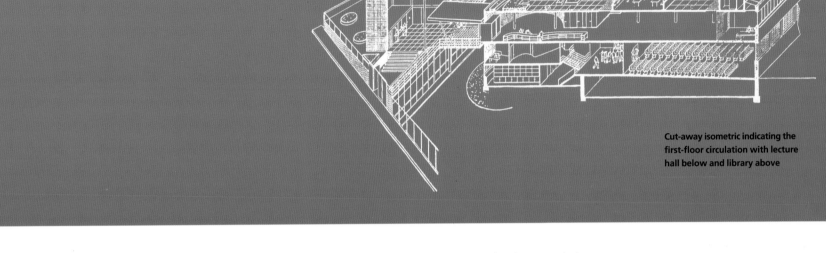

Cut-away isometric indicating the first-floor circulation with lecture hall below and library above

Between 1926 and 1933 Le Corbusier realized three separate works for the French branch of the Salvation Army. The first, a four-story, 104-bed annex to the Palais du Peuple in 1926 was raised on two-story-high *pilotis* on a back lot in the rue des Cordeliers. The second was the Asile Flottant of 1929, an eighty-meter-long (262-foot) concrete barge moored on the Seine at the Quai d'Austerlitz that was converted into a 130-bed "floating asylum." The last and largest was this once majestic structure known as the Cité de Refuge. Comprising a seven-story slab block, inserted onto an irregular site, it was built to accommodate five hundred to six hundred beds and a variety of social services.

The project went through four preliminary versions, each one more ingenious than the next, before it attained its final form. This final iteration comprised a narrow, totally glazed slab lining the northern boundary of the site with three auxiliary structures in the form of Platonic solids set in front of the slab to the south. These last comprise a portico in the form of an open cube, a cylindrical reception hall faced in ceramic tiles and glass blocks, and a parallelepiped accommodating a general foyer at grade, a library/lounge above, and a 270-seat auditorium below. A key aspect of the spatial experience of the Cité de Refuge was the consecutive flow of volumes as one proceeds through the building, with the visitor entering under the portico and crossing a short footbridge to approach the cylindrical entry hall. Inside, one passes a curvilinear reception desk to ascend via a simple stair to the second-floor library, which

opens onto a circular terrace furnished with geometrical, concrete planters. The terrace is now unused, its planters having been replaced by trees and the library turned into offices.

The main patron for all three Salvation Army commissions was Princess de Polignac (née Winaretta Singer, heir to the Singer sewing machine fortune), who dedicated a considerable amount of her personal wealth to the Salvation Army. How Le Corbusier first made contact with this benefactress remains obscure, although architectural historian Brian Brace Taylor has suggested that he may have met her through his composer–brother, Albert Jeanneret, with whom he was in the habit of attending fashionable *soirées musicales.*[7] Le Corbusier and the princess shared similar ideals when it came to social reform, including a belief in social welfare and the general beneficial effects of sanitary, well-organized, modern living conditions.

Le Corbusier already had experienced firsthand the *dom kommuna,* or communal housing, of the young Soviet state during a visit he made to Russia in 1928. Among the avant-garde works he would have seen on this occasion was the experimental Narkomfin collective dwelling block in Moscow that, designed by his Russian colleague Mosei Ginzburg, was then under construction. The program for the Cité de Refuge provided a range of residential and communal facilities even more comprehensive than the Narkomfin communal dwelling. Separate dining halls for men and women were housed on the raised ground floor, served by a kitchen that was supplied

5.57

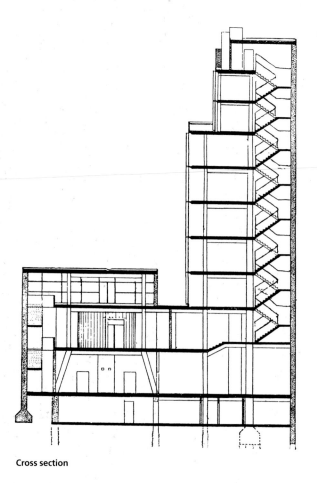

Crossatle

Cross section

by an internal driveway ingeniously woven into the plan of the basement. The principal slab was similarly divided according to gender, with men allocated to the eastern half and women to the western half, where they could take advantage of both eastern and western views. Special rooms were originally provided on several floors for mothers with children while the fifth floor was equipped with separate collective dormitories for infants and older children. The opaque northern wall on each level contained the necessary toilets and showers, small offices for nurses and superintendents, and milk preparation and drying rooms. (From today's perspective, it is remarkable how well the needs of single mothers and children were accommodated.) On the sixth floor, a small, "symbolic" office was provided for the Princess de Polignac while on the seventh and eighth floors, set back from the southern facade, were modest apartments for the director and the assistant director. The basement accommodated large top-lit workshops of irregular shape, as well as a clothing store and disinfecting rooms, with these last directly accessed by a separate stair leading down from the dispensary beneath the cylindrical entrance.

While the Cité de Refuge was one of the most ingeniously organized public buildings of Le Corbusier's prewar career, its technical shortcomings were nothing short of tragic. Unfortunately, excessively deep pile foundations had to be sunk in order to find solid ground for the structure, a necessity that consumed a disproportionate amount of the budget. The consequence was that the double-glazed curtain wall planned for the southern facade had to be reduced

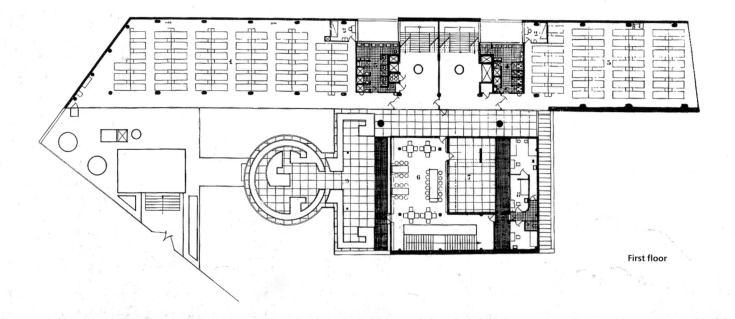

First floor

to a single sheet. This in turn meant that the air-conditioning system originally envisaged for the entire volume could not be fully realized. Without sufficient cooling, the dormitory rooms overheated during the summer while a lack of ventilation meant that the air was stagnant and unhealthy.

It is a measure of the daring inventiveness of Le Corbusier and Pierre Jeanneret that they constantly overreached themselves technically. Fully air-conditioned, hermetically sealed, curtain-walled structures were totally unknown in France in 1933, and even today, some seventy years later, they are still something of a rarity. Neither the French building industry nor the architects or their consultants were quite up to designing and executing such a high-tech building. This much is forcibly brought home by the shallow *brise soleil* that were among several modifications superimposed on the southern face of the building in 1952, when Jeanneret was commissioned to restore the badly deteriorated, war-damaged structure. In contrast to the Immeuble Clarté, which they had realized a year earlier in Geneva, the Cité de Refuge was ultimately unable to prove itself as a pioneering work in curtain-wall construction.

5.61

Interior views of the entry sequence

Immeuble Clarté

Geneva, Switzerland, 1930–33

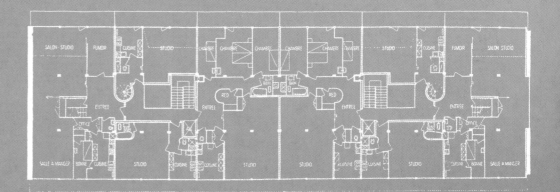

Typical floor plan

In the Geneva industrialist Edmund Wanner, Le Corbusier finally found his ideal "captain of industry": the mythical, Henry Ford–like personage that he evoked in his 1923 book *Towards a New Architecture* as the only figure capable of taking responsibility for society's welfare in the emerging Machine Age. The two may have first met at the Exposition des Arts Décoratifs in Paris in 1925. Wanner and Le Corbusier first began to collaborate two years later after encountering each other again at the Werbund Weissenhoffsiedlung in Stuttgart. This seminal housing exhibition organized by Ludwig Mies van der Rohe featured twenty-one houses by leading German and international architects such as Peter Behrens, Walter Gropius, Bruno Taut, J. J. P. Oud, and Mart Stam, as well as Le Corbusier and Pierre Jeanneret, who, as Atelier 35S, realized two model houses on the site.

The Atelier 35S's first design for Wanner was the so-called Project Wanner, a development of seven-story apartment blocks situated close to Alfred Betrand Park in Geneva. These units were designed to be made of prefabricated metal parts and erected by semi-skilled workers, thereby eliminating the multiplicity of trades that then – as now – were one of the factors inhibiting the industrialization of the building industry. The project was abandoned, but Wanner followed it with a commission to build this nine-story block of forty-nine apartments in the Eaux Vives quarter of Geneva.

While Wanner was an extremely demanding client, he had considerable technical resources at his disposal. Even more important, he was capable of financing his own projects. He headed the family metal-fabricating business (Serrurie de Batiment), which had been founded by his grandfather. He was extremely interested in creating whole buildings out of metal, from their basic structural frame to their smallest details. The Geneva apartment block was to be fabricated from arc-welded steel, with hollow steel columns and transoms and I-section steel beams supporting wooden floor joists. Except for double layers of brickwork separating the apartments, cement roofing, and the plaster applied to battens lining the walls and the ceilings, this building was assembled from methods of construction that were entirely dry. It was Le Corbusier's first venture into what he later called *maison à sec*.[8]

Wanner's company was able to fabricate all the secondary metalwork with great precision, including the exterior sun blinds, the flush-faced roller shutters, the steel-framed, double-glazed sliding windows (which ran on a ball-bearing system patented by Wanner), steel-tube balustrading filled with wire mesh, and welded spiral stairs, the treads of which were cantilevered off a single steel tube. The most prominent and daring metal construction in the Immeuble Clarté are the top-lit, steel-framed, principal access stairs, the treads

and landings of which were filled with large glass blocks of a similar order as the smaller glass blocks lining the building's entrance halls, with both kinds of lenses assuring the luminosity that gives the building its name.

The building is set at an angle to the street grid in order to gain a more advantageous orientation for the apartments on either side of the block. There are eight apartments on each floor of varying size and plan. The arrangement of these units, some of which are double-height duplexes, is remarkably ingenious given the size of the building and the fact that the entire circulation, apart from the independent entry halls within each unit, turns on the carefully calculated placement of the internal stairs that serve the duplexes. Six large duplexes with eight rooms, each fed by dogleg stairs, are situated on two floors at either end of the building while the six three-room duplexes in the middle are served by spiral stairs. All of these double-height units are on the southwestern side of the building. Four-room apartments with exposures on both sides sit between the duplexes; they are joined on the northeastern side by single-room studios. The ground-floor podium accommodates garages, entry halls, and some professional space. The set-back top floor is comprised of five units – two three-room apartments, two six-room, and one five-room.

The Immeuble Clarté (along with the Cité de Refuge) helped pioneer curtain wall construction. In this instance, however, the all-glass facade was shaded when necessary not only by external roller blinds and shutters but also by one-and-a-half-meter-deep balconies that ran the length of the building on both sides – every other floor. These balconies, decked with wood planking, were carried on light steel brackets cantilevered off the main frame. Each apartment's balcony was divided from its neighbor by steel-framed, frosted glass panels rising to just above eye level.

The Immeuble Clarté also marks Le Corbusier's first use of a steel frame, a structural form that he continued to explore with the Pavillon Suisse in the Cité Universitaire in Paris. These buildings were departures from his Five Points of a New Architecture, which were dependent on the structural continuity of a reinforced concrete and cantilevered slab construction. In the Immeuble Clarté the free plan is still present, but as in the Villa Stein de Monzie, there are no *pilotis* and the facade is not strictly speaking free since it is absolutely contiguous with the steel frame.

Twice restored since it was built more than seventy years ago, the Immeuble Clarté remains a much sought after address. It is without a doubt one of the finest modern buildings realized in Geneva in the twentieth century and one of the most important apartment buildings realized anywhere in the years between the world wars.

6.67

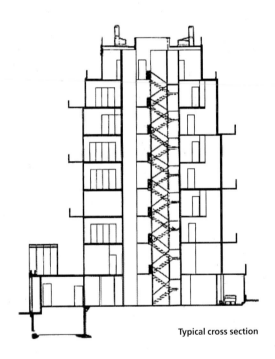

Typical cross section

Detailing of the restored building
with multi-layered sun screening

One of the building's two principal
porticoes and the interior of one of
its entry lobbies

Detail of the access stair and
gallery fitted with glass treads

Pavillon Suisse, Cité Universitaire

Paris, 1930–32

Perspective showing ground-floor common room at the rear of the building

The Pavillon Suisse at the Cité Universitaire in Paris is in many ways an extremely modest structure, just five stories tall and containing forty-five dorm rooms and a small communal space. The commission for this prestigious project came after the disqualification of Le Corbusier's project for the 1927 League of Nations competition. Although the Le Corbusier and Pierre Jeanneret project was one of several finalists premiated for the Société des Nations, when a more traditional design was finally chosen, it was said to include aspects borrowed from Le Corbusier's design. At the initiative of Professor René Feuter of Zurich (who would later commission a small house from Le Corbusier), and with the subsequent support of Sigfried Giedion, Karl Moser, and Raoul La Roche, the federation of Swiss universities was persuaded to award him the commission for the Pavillon Suisse. According to Deborah Gans, this was informally regarded in Swiss circles as being some kind of compensation for the underhanded way he had been treated in 1927.[9]

The Pavillon Suisse was one of several buildings that served, in part, as prototypes for the residential slabs Le Corbusier had conceived as the basic dwelling units of his ideal city, that is to say, the *blocs à redent* of his ideal city that he set before the public in the 1935 book *La Ville Radieuse.* The Cité de Refuge and the Immeuble Clarté preceded it as examples, but with square openings running along the north elevation of the block and a curtain wall entirely covering its southern face, the Pavillon Suisse may be seen as the ultimate prototype for such a residential block.

All of the Pavillon Suisse's forty-five student rooms are housed in a light steel frame structure, resting on the concrete substructure. The remainder of the building could have hardly been more simple. It comprised an elevator/stair tower attached to its northern face, an entrance foyer, a reading room, a kitchenette, a director's office, and a small caretaker's apartment at grade level. The curtain wall was largely furnished by Edmund Wanner metalworks, including the patented sliding steel windows. The building incorporated several technical innovations in addition to this curtain wall, including the reinforced concrete platform and the steel frame of the dormitory wing. The northern elevation was clad in precast cement slabs laid over brick and separated by a two-inch air space from the insulating block on the interior face. There were other innovations applied to the interior, such as the subdividing walls between the students' rooms with wood-framed, sound-insulating sandwich construction.

As in the Cité de Refuge, the architects were again hampered by the poor bearing capacity of the soil. They were thus compelled to sink six pairs of concrete piles up to sixty-five feet into the ground. This led them to superimpose the main body of the building on a reinforced concrete platform supported by twin reinforced concrete beams, which in turn transferred the load onto six pairs of extra-massive concrete *pilotis*. The architects' use of *pilotis,* together with the paved threshold to the building, also allowed them to create a particularly powerful, sculptural undercroft beneath the block,

7.72

General view of the front block in
the mid-1950s

General view of the rear
of the building soon after its
completion in 1932

General view of the main approach
to the block today, after a complete
renovation of the main façade

of a kind that would reformulate in the Unité d'Habitation, built in Marseilles twenty years later.

Le Corbusier and Jeanneret took a Neo-Cubist approach to architectural composition in both the Cité de Refuge and the Pavillon Suisse. In each instance, the slab is conceived as though it were a layered "picture plane." At the Cité de Refuge, objects are arranged in varying depth in front of this surface. In the Pavillon Suisse, the concave concrete wall of the stair tower and the parallel concave rubble-stone wall of the reading room are situated as figurative forms behind the plane of the slab. Where the Cité de Refuge disposed of Platonic forms in front of a slab on an irregular site, here the free form of the stair tower and the reading room is more organic. Similarly, the main stair curves out into the center of the foyer against the airfoil section of a central chimney shaft. In the common areas we may say that the "free plan" becomes reversed where in the Villa Stein de Monzie the columns conform to a Palladian grid and the subdividing planes remain free of the structure, here both the columns of the reading room and the glazed

wall, separating this space from the foyer, follow each other in a three-dimensional relief that echoes the concave wall of the reading room. These organic gestures anticipate the "visual acoustics" he will return to in the Chapel of Nôtre Dame-du-Haut in Ronchamp. This organic display was metaphorically enhanced in the Pavillon Suisse by a photographic mural of minerals, crystals, and fossils pasted onto the curved surfaces of the chimney shaft and the back wall of the reading room.

Although the Pavillon Suisse as it stands today retains its initial brilliance, it has seen a number of changes over the years, above all with regard to its surrounding context. The Cité Universitaire campus has expanded around the building to such an extent that the plastic implications of its freestanding form have been largely compromised. The original curtain wall was reconstructed with double glazing, sacrificing much of the original tautness. And in 1948, during a postwar renovation, Le Corbusier replaced the original photographic mural with a multicolored collage that includes, among other icons, the image of a winged goat cradled by a giant hand.[10]

7.74

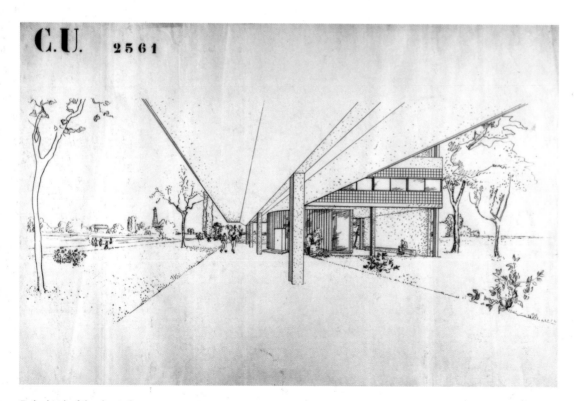

Early sketch of the elevated slab block with *piloti* and common room at the rear

Detail of Le Corbusier's 1948 mural
in the common room

The common room with
furniture by Pierre Jeanneret,
Charlotte Perriand, and
Le Corbusier

A view of the main foyer from
the common room

Interiors of a typical
student's room

Immeuble Porte Molitor / Appartement Le Corbusier

Paris, 1933

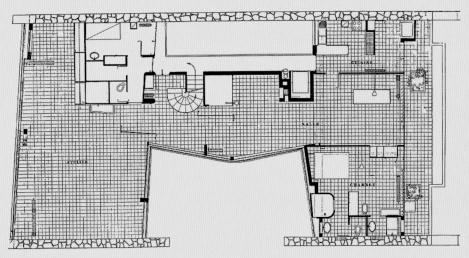

Plan of the lower floor of Le Corbusier's two-story apartment and studio, situated at the top of the building

Le Corbusier and Pierre Jeanneret designed this speculative, eight-story apartment building for an emerging bourgeois neighborhood then under development. Le Corbusier managed to reserve the top floor for his own residence and studio. One of the most elegant aspects of the Porte Molitor block is the orchestration of its plate glass and glass-block facade fronting onto the rue Nungesser et Coli. Apart from the Immeuble Clarté's, it is Le Corbusier's most sophisticated curtain wall of the period. The fenestration and balcony patterns subtly change from floor to floor as the building rises. The first floor has a continuous shallow terrace with a glass balustrade running the full width of the block; the second floor is equipped with an equally shallow terrace set in from the cross-walls and protected by a balustrade of gridded steel. The two floors above this are equipped with bay windows and glass-block spandrels. The uppermost glass-block spandrel of the composition serves as the balustrade to the fifth-floor apartment's terrace. The sixth and seventh floors, set back from the front of the building, are glazed with sliding and fixed glass panels for the full width of the block. The influence of Pierre Chareau's Maison de Verre (1930–32) is patently manifest in this facade, Le Corbusier having made regular visits to this all-glass house during its construction in the rue St. Guillanne in the center of Paris.

The ground floor of the Porte Molitor building is subtly handled in both plan and elevation; the displacement of the main entrance to the left of a central, freestanding column permits access to small ground-floor apartments left and right while opening up to the fluidity of the top-lit foyer. This condensation of the free plan anticipates a similar opposition between freestanding columns and partitions in the organization of the apartments above – a play that is curiously absent in Le Corbusier's eighth-floor penthouse. The internal organization of the floors depended on the displacement of the middle support in a line of five columns running between the party walls. This displacement permitted a generous elevator lobby throughout, with equally ample thresholds for each apartment. With a narrow service court facing south and a main light well facing north, each apartment receives ample light and was well served according to the standards of the time, along with a service elevator providing direct access to each kitchen. Ten "maid's rooms" also were provided on the ground floor and basement, with the lower tier being lit by another light court.

The location of the servants' quarters (traditionally sited in the top floor) allowed Le Corbusier to take full advantage of being on top of the building. In the first place, he could build up into the attic under the zoning regulations; in the second, he could gain more space by omitting the passenger elevator on his floor. Thus, there is no honorific approach to his penthouse – one gains access by walking up the service stair and entering from the service gallery. This casual approach is compensated for by a generous entrance hall that acquires almost monumental proportions by virtue of two large pivoting doors. These doors function as "valves," isolating

8.82

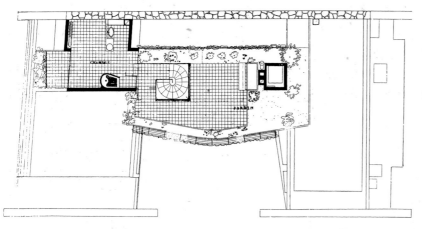

Plan of the upper floor of
Le Corbusier's apartment and
roof terrace

Detail of service gallery

either the apartment or the studio or both. When closed, these doors secure both the studio and the apartment and lead the eye upward to the sky as one follows the line of the spiral stair rising to the roof terrace. When both the doors are open, the space runs freely from the studio on the west to the dining room on the east.

Le Corbusier's painting studio is the most magnificent space in the apartment, its vaulted concrete ceiling rising high into the attic space. The character of this room is determined by the light coming in from the west via a skylight, as well as by the unplastered rubble-stone party wall that runs the full width of the studio. A small study sits to the south of this double-height space. The apartment's elongated living space terminates in a shallow, vaulted dining area set before a terrace that runs the full width of the building. To the right of this room, passing through a pivoting closet-wall, one comes upon the master bedroom, which is equipped with a water closet, a bidet, and two separate shower spaces. In many respects, these last are the most idiosyncratic features of the plan. Their highly plastic, not to say organic, forms, painted white, are handled as though they were elements abstracted from the Aegean Islands or from the vernacular forms of the Baleric Islands. After the realization of this work, Le Corbusier would live and paint here for the rest of his life, that is, until his death in 1965. Today, while the entire apartment belongs to the Foundation Le Corbusier, an appropriate, semipublic use for it has yet to be established.

8.83

Entry foyer of the apartment
of Le Corbusier

The spiral stair serving the
roof terrace of Le Corbusier's
apartment

8.86

Le Corbusier's studio

Detail of kitchen

View of bathroom from
the bedroom

The guest bedroom

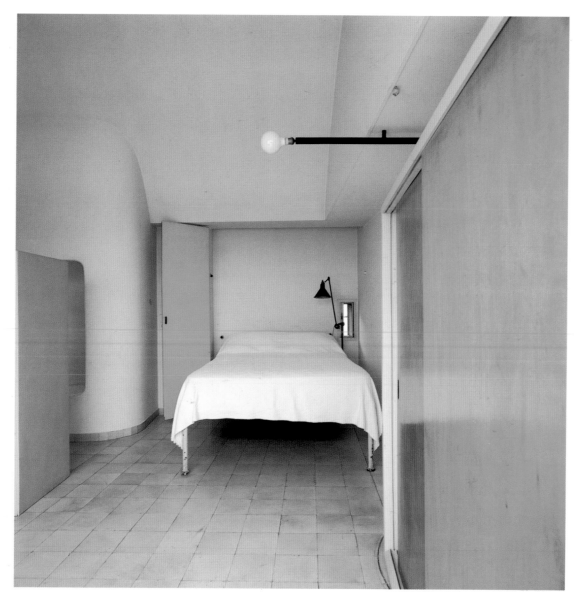

The main bedroom

Unité d'Habitation de Marseilles

Marseilles, France, 1945–52

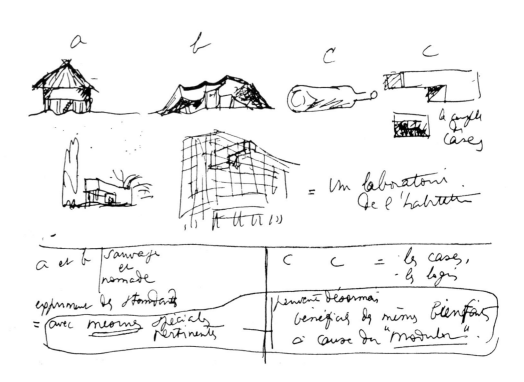

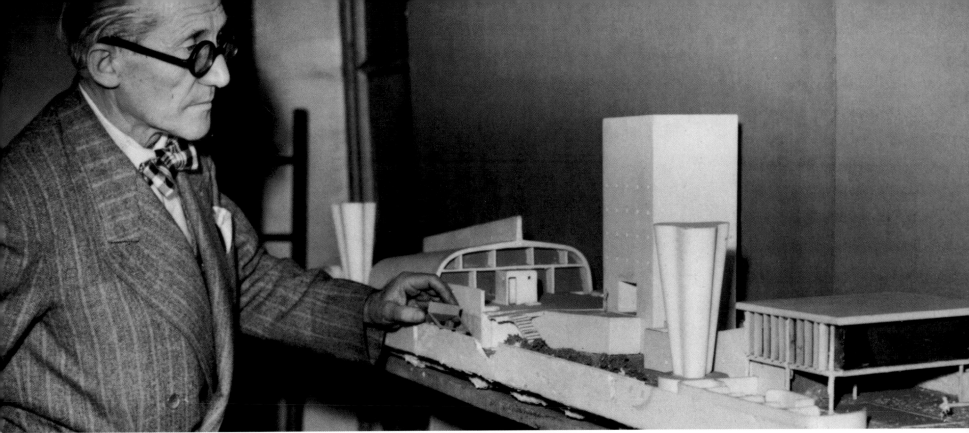

There is perhaps no other mid-century housing block that was carried out with such conviction as the Unité d'Habitation in Marseilles. Forty-nine years after it opened, this remarkable structure still looks like a stranded transatlantic liner as it looms into view above the trees of the Boulevard Michelet. It hovers above its parklike setting as though it were the apotheosis of the modern project, the concrete realization of the possibilities felt during a brief euphoric moment in Europe after the end of World War II. This utopian vision, first projected in 1945 at the behest of Raoul Dautry, the then French minister of reconstruction, is one of the most singular achievements of Le Corbusier's fertile career. The Unité represents a synthesis of all the housing studies that he had made during the previous three decades as he tried to evolve a form of collective dwelling that could respond to the "housing question" at an appropriate scale.

The Unité's physical characteristics are more immediately apparent than its social goals. One circumnavigates this massive, exquisitely proportioned, reinforced concrete slab block transfixed by its polychromed facade and by the sublime profiles of its Egyptoid *pilotis* that support, seemingly without effort, the building's massively canted undercroft. The block carried by these *pilotis* is 450 feet long, 79 feet deep, and 184 feet tall. The base serves as an "artificial ground" within which is housed a monumental entry hall, its presence indicated by a cantilevered *porte cochere* projecting well beyond the limits of the slab. Under this canopy, a battery of frameless plate glass doors gives one the sense of French technological prowess at its best. Much the same quality pervades the various facilities that penetrate the semipublic fabric of the building, including the elevator shafts, escape stairs, wide internal streets, and, above all, the double-height communal shopping floor and hotel suspended at midpoint in the height of the slab. Both services are still in operation a half-century after the building's inauguration.

The Unité comprises 337 apartments of twenty-three different types, ranging from units for bachelors and childless couples to those for families with up to eight children. Many of the units are duplexes, which interlock with the internal street by virtue of passing either over or under it. A typical three-bedroom apartment is twelve feet wide and features a double-height living room measuring just over fifteen feet from floor to ceiling. The duplexes that pass over the internal street would appear to be the more convenient since one enters directly into the kitchen and dining/living space. From there a stair ascends to the parents' bedroom on the mezzanine overlooking the double-height living volume. Children's bedrooms are situated at this mezzanine level on the same floor on the opposite side of the block. The down-going units are more promiscuous in terms of spatial arrangement. One enters from the internal street into a kitchen/dining space situated on a mezzanine suspended over the double-height living room. One descends to a living/sleeping space for the parents and from there passes to the children's bedrooms at the back on the other side of the block.

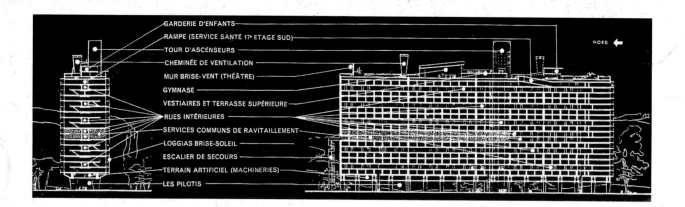

GARDERIE D'ENFANTS
RAMPE (SERVICE SANTÉ 17ᵉ ETAGE SUD)
TOUR D'ASCÉNSEURS
CHEMINÉE DE VENTILATION
MUR BRISE-VENT (THÉÂTRE)
GYMNASE
VESTIAIRES ET TERRASSE SUPÉRIEURE
RUES INTÉRIEURES
SERVICES COMMUNS DE RAVITAILLEMENT
LOGGIAS BRISE-SOLEIL
ESCALIER DE SECOURS
TERRAIN ARTIFICIEL (MACHINERIES)
LES PILOTIS

NORD ←

Schematic cross and long sections showing the distribution of different communal services throughout the building

Main driveway approach to the rear of the building

9.94

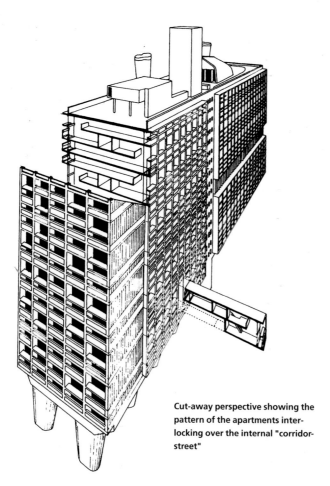

Cut-away perspective showing the
pattern of the apartments interlocking over the internal "corridor-
street"

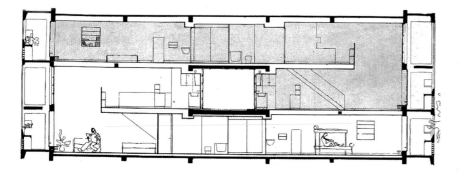

Typical cross-over apartment
section: the shaded floor is an up-
going unit; the un-shaded is
down-going in respect of entry
from the internal street

Almost all of these standard, interlocking duplex units are oriented east–west, with some living rooms facing inland toward the mountains and others facing out toward the sea. Each unit has an ample inset balcony and thus is shaded to varying degrees by the soffit above and by the projecting cross-walls. These fixed, large-scale *brise soleil* are polychromed in a syncopated manner so as to give an alternating color identity to each unit when seen from the surrounding park. The roof of the Unité is a kind of miniacropolis, providing a series of social services in a world that is patently set apart from the hustle and bustle of everyday life. It accommodates a running track, a belvedere, a children's wading pool, and a series of small, freestanding structures, including an auditorium, a nursery school, and a gymnasium.

Never was the ideal of a new universal standard for modern housing so convincingly and thoroughly realized as in this work. While Le Corbusier would build four other Unité blocks – at Rezé-lès-Nantes (1952), Briey en Forêt (1956), Berlin (1957), and Firminy-Vert (1960) – none of these matched the generosity of the initial project, largely because of their drastically reduced budgets. Much of today's urban sprawl, which has consumed vast domains of the pre-1945 landscape, could have been avoided had such a prototype been consciously adopted throughout the developed world. Le Corbusier himself was fond of contrasting the 1,722 square feet of land that served as open space surrounding the Unité to the 4,844 square feet required by an equivalent population accommodated in freestanding suburban houses. The Marseilles Unité stands as the major testament to a particularly hopeful but brief postwar epoch. The fact that it is still occupied today testifies to the validity of the original concept. Still, it is important to note that the precise manner and scale at which the idea was carried out were crucial to its success. Reduced versions of this idea that would be repeated ad infinitum around the outskirts of European cities testify to the way in which the scale and scope of an originally heroic concept could not be transposed into a bureaucratically reduced program for expedient urban development.

Pages 102–103: Two views of the interiors of the mid-block shopping street

Roof terrace with ventilating stacks and the shell concrete roof of the gymnasium

Interior of a typical duplex apartment and balcony

Chapel of Nôtre Dame-du-Haut

Ronchamp, France, 1950–55

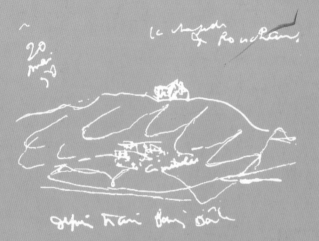

Le Corbusier's sketch of the site's
pre-existing ruined church

When Le Corbusier was first approached to design the Chapel of Nôtre Dame-du-Haut at Ronchamp, his impulse was to decline. His project for a shrine of Mary Magdalene in La Sainte Baume had been rejected a few years before, and he had come to regard the Church as a dead institution. Undeterred, two religious leaders, Canon Lucien Ledeur and Père Alain Couturier, urged him to accept the challenge. "We do not have much to offer you," Ledeur told him, "but we do have this: a wonderful setting and the possibility to go all the way. I do not know whether you are committed to building churches, but if you should build one, then the conditions offered by Ronchamp are ideal. This is not a lost cause: you will be given free rein to create what you will."

Le Corbusier used this free rein to create the most sculptural work of his entire career. He also exploited the extraordinary qualities of the site. The chapel is positioned at the peak of a large hill, affording spectacular views toward the foothills of the Vosges Mountains to the north and the Jura Mountains to the south. The site provided Le Corbusier with an opportunity to engage in what he called "visual acoustics," that is to say, a large-scale sculptural game in which the concave and convex forms of the building swept out into the landscape in such a way as to echo the surrounding topography. Thus, the curved outline of the building in plan was a response to the profile of the aforementioned mountain ranges.

Ronchamp was an auspicious site not only because of the attendant panorama but also because of its long history as a sacred place, serving as a sun temple in prehistoric times, as a Christian sanctuary in the fourth century, and as a church site from the twelfth century on. The previous church on this site was destroyed during World War II, but the location continued to serve as a place of pilgrimage. The chapel was conceived from the outset as the culmination of an annual pilgrimage route attended by up to thirty thousand of the faithful. These pilgrims arrive at the "templum" via an informal propylaea made up of a pilgrims' dormitory and a caretaker's house, both of reinforced concrete construction with grass-covered roofs. The templum is implicitly contained by these bunkerlike structures and, at the northeast corner of the site, by a small, stepped ziggurat built out of the rubble of the previous chapel, thereby commemorating those who lost their lives defending the crest of the hill toward the end of the war.

The focus of this acropolis is the chapel itself, whose dramatically curved roof caps the whitewashed structure like an upswept concrete wing. One of the most amazing aspects of this building is how its size seems to vary according to one's position. From certain aspects it appears to be rather large whereas from others it assumes a more modest scale that is closer to its actual dimensions. This alternating "monumentality" is apparent when approaching from

The main approach

10.106

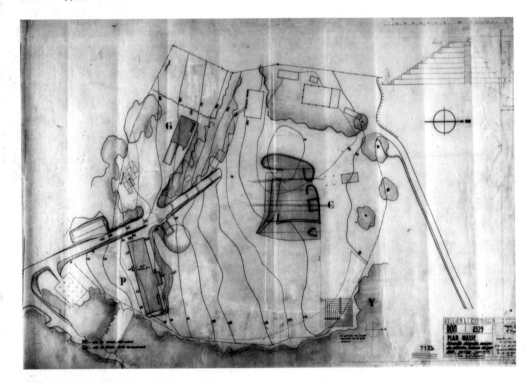

Site plan

the south, where the concrete roof appears as an enormous can-tilevered mass suspended over the curved and canted southern wall. This heavy form also appears to float above the wall due to a small gap that is established between the wall and the roof.

The visitor is made instantly aware that the building has been con-ceived in terms of the landscape, above all by the roughly-plastered southern wall that sweeps out with tremendous force toward the horizon. This striking gesture is answered on the eastern face by a concave wall that, while cradling the exterior altar and pul-pit, also embraces the open-air sanctuary of the grass forecourt. The external sanctum is raised on a shallow podium faced in stone and furnished with a number of solid prisms, including a stone altar, and a thin wooden cross of unusually anthropomor-phic proportions.

The double curve of the chapel's concrete roof was supposedly derived from a crab shell that Le Corbusier found on a beach in Long Island, New York. It is also equally reminiscent of an air-foil section, and in this regard it can be seen to derive from the catenary curve of the suspended canvas roof of Le Corbusier's Pavillon des Temps Nouveaux erected in 1936 for the 1937 Paris International Exposition. At the same time this improbable levitating roof is carried on rough-plastered masonry walls that evoke the whitewashed vernacular of the Mediterranean.

The chapel is at its most intimate on its northern and western faces, particularly where one enters informally from the north between the back-to-back light cowls of the western and eastern side chapels, which rise above the saddleback profile of the roof. The intimate character of this facade stems from spot fenestra-tion of the sacristy and from the all but domestic scale of the con-crete stair serving the priest's offices above. If the northern face is domestic, the western end is cryptically symbolic. Here the inclined roof, curtailed by a bounding parapet, drains through a double-barreled concrete gargoyle into an oval concrete cistern beneath. The rough concrete wall of this basin is in strong formal contrast to the concrete pyramid and cylinder set within its perim-eter. The harsh character of these concrete elements combines with the slight protrusion of the confessionals at the western end of the nave to constitute a surreal assembly of elements that are surely more pagan than Christian in their general aura.

The drama of the chapel's interior derives in large measure from two countervailing inclines: the floor of the nave falling east, toward the altar, and that of the sanctum counterinclined toward the west. These slopes, in conjunction with the stone-paved axis that indicates the orientation of the nave, impart a dynamic character to an interior whose overall scale fluctuates as much as that of the building's exterior. The southern face, punctuated by seemingly random openings filled with clear and tinted glass, assumes a cathedral-like aura while the diminutive western end has a more forbidding character, imparted by wooden confessionals set side by side on the nave's central axis.

The contrast between the chapel's gray concrete roof, floor, and pulpit and its whitewashed walls is heightened by the way light enters the space. The overall illumination of the chapel is provided by deeply set, multicolored windows in the southern wall, by starlike perforations in the choir wall, and by a narrow, vertical, louvered window between the two. Constantly varying levels of light also enter the nave via the three side chapels, which receive light from the north, east, and west, respectively. While the cowl of the largest side chapel opens toward the north, the two smaller, semicylindrical side chapels are flooded with light at sunrise and sunset – the colored shaft of the eastern cowl glowing deep red at dawn while the inner surface of the western cowl turns gold with the last rays of the sun.

When a visitor arrives at this acropolis from the south, he is immediately struck by the brightly colored, enameled metal door. This emblematic plane pivots on its axis to admit honorific processionals on feast days. Covered with a set of different interlocking, multicolored motifs inside and out, this heraldic panel enriches the relatively somber interior of the nave, the gray, white, and slate tones of which are relieved by wooden pews carved by Le Corbusier's sculptor–colleague Joseph Savina. The angular arrangement of these pews, elevated on a shallow wood-block platform and contained by a concrete curb, recalls the work of Carlo Scarpa, as does much of the other detailing. This is particularly true of the altar rail, the crucifix, and the triangular steel candelabra, all of which display especially sensitive profiles and proportions.

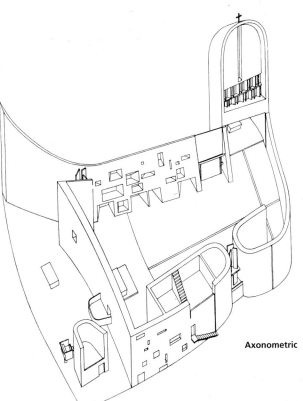

Axonometric

10.109

Interior

10.110

10.114

Le Corbusier. 1911. Sketches of the lighting principle in the Serapeum of the Villa Adriana at Tivoli, near Rome. Drawn by the architect during his *Voyage d'Orient*

Two views from the northeast

10.115

10.116

Detail of the southern light cowl

View of the chapel from the
west showing the double-barreled
gargoyle that drains the roof

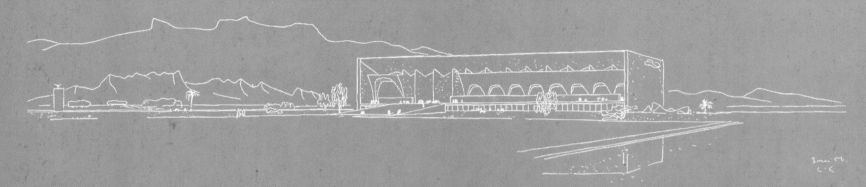

Chandigarh, Capital of the Punjab

Chandigarh, India, 1950–68

Le Corbusier in Chandigarh

11.120

In 1950, at the age of sixty-three, Le Corbusier found himself working at the highest level for a society that was still largely preindustrial by designing the city and major governmental buildings of Chandigarh, the new capital of the Punjab. When India gained its independence from Britain in 1947, the governing treaty dictated that the western portion of Punjab, including its capital, Lahore, be ceded to the new country of Pakistan. The immediate need for a new Punjabi capital provided Le Corbusier with an opportunity to design a major government complex, an ambition that had been thwarted two decades earlier when his entry for the League of Nations competition had been summarily disqualified.

Thus, Le Corbusier concentrated most of his energy on the design of the capitol buildings, representing the center of power. Otherwise, his overall urban plan would not differ that much from the layout projected by his predecessors, a design team headed by Polish-American architect Matthew Nowicki, whose death in a plane crash was the occasion for giving the commission to Le Corbusier. Le Corbusier followed Nowicki in placing the capitol complex to the north of the city, where it was set against the profile of the Himalayan Mountains. He conceived this arrangement in humanist terms as an analogue to the human body in which the capitol was the head and the cultural institutions were the intellect, while the road layout functioned as the circulation system.

Early sketches of the capitol showing the way in which many of the forms were inspired by the landscape and by Indian cattle

The site on the sparsely settled Punjab plain was selected by the Punjabi chief engineer P. L. Varma, who was impressed by its audacious grandeur. Named after Chandi, the Hindu goddess of power, the building of the city was emblematic of Prime Minister Jawaharlal Nehru's new India. Le Corbusier's capitol would comprise three major buildings: the Assembly, the High Court, and the Secretariat. Its composition can be compared in certain respects to a Mayan acropolis, where monumental structures are invariably situated according to auspicious alignments against vast natural backdrops. The three honorific structures were distinguished from each other through the use of large sculptural elements, the specific form of which Le Corbusier was to adduce from the flora and fauna of the Indian landscape. These forms were augmented by tectonic elements executed in shell concrete construction; a parasol, a frustum, and a hyperbolic vault. These features, together with his habitual *brise soleil,* were orchestrated and articulated in such a way as to provide each building with a distinctive character.

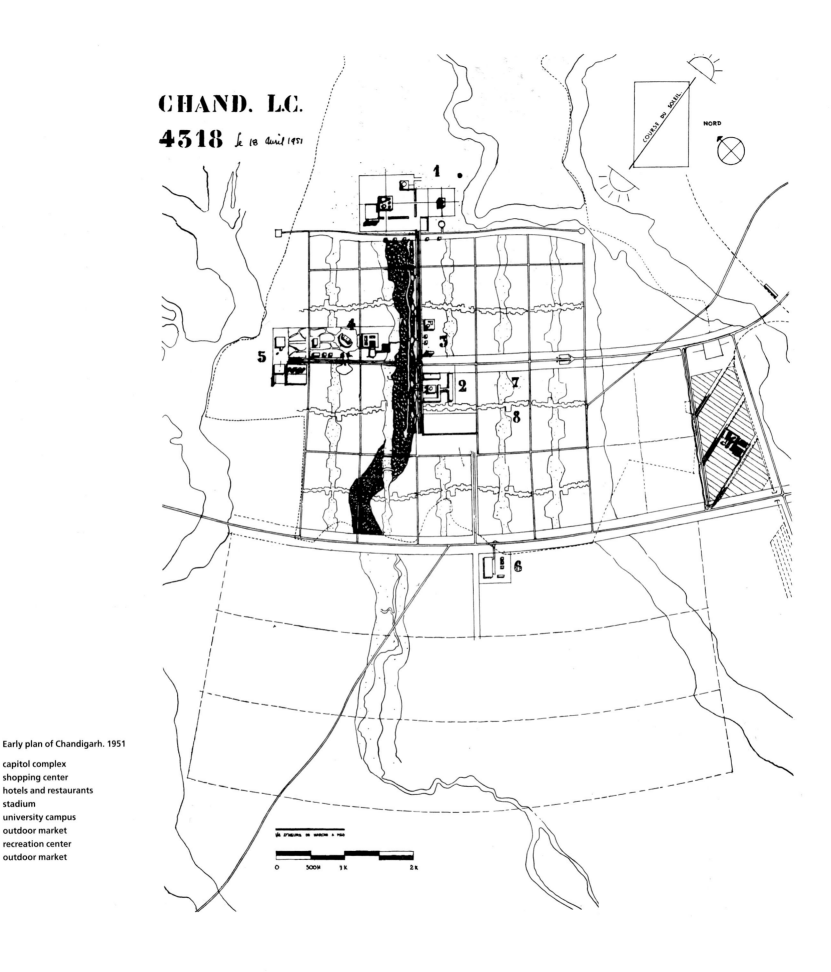

CHAND. LC.
4318 le 18 avril 1951

1

COURSE DU SOLEIL

NORD

11.121

Early plan of Chandigarh. 1951

1 capitol complex
2 shopping center
3 hotels and restaurants
4 stadium
5 university campus
6 outdoor market
7 recreation center
8 outdoor market

0   500M   1K   2K

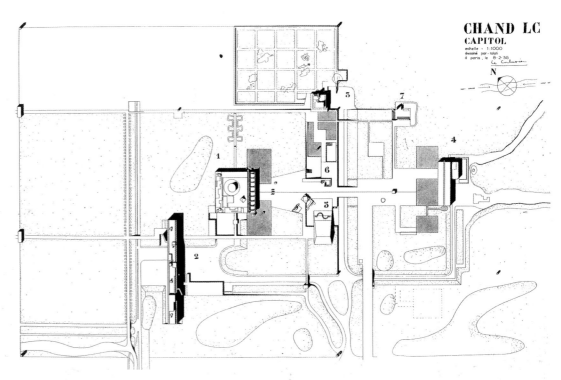

General and close-up views
of the High Court

Site plan showing the principal
monuments

1 Assembly
2 Secretariat
3 Governor's Palace
4 High Court
5 Fosse of Consideration
6 Multi-level garden to
   the Governor's Palace
7 Open Hand

The relatively low prism of the Assembly, with its closely set *brise soleil,* was distinguished from the other two structures by its dynamic roof profile, comprising an elevator tower, a pyramid, and, to one side, a concrete "cooling tower" set on the top of the circular assembly chamber. This frustum form served as a kind of surrogate dome. In addition to providing zenithal light to the chamber beneath, it also functioned as an observation platform, accessed via a steel *passarelle* attached to the elevator shaft.

The entrance to the building was shaded by a concrete portico that extended the full width of the structure. Taking the form of an enormous gutter, its concrete blade walls were pierced with irregular holes. The canted section of this enormous canopy seems to have been partially inspired by the profile of Indian cattle. Le Corbusier displayed comparable virtuosity in the convex interior of the parliamentary chamber, which was lined with organically shaped, acoustical "clouds" attached to the inner surface of the frustum. This hyperbolic cone was set within a hypostyle hall of thin concrete columns that served as the milling space around the chamber and created an interior volume reminiscent of a mosque.

The vertical *brise soleil* of the Assembly was formally countered by the horizontal sun-screening of the Secretariat. Here the *brise soleil* pattern produced a syncopated rhythm across the southeastern face of the building. This rhythm was interrupted about a third of the way along the facade by a fugal interplay of deep, double-height balconies, which indicated the point at which this 250-meter-long (830-foot) facade was supposed to be entered. As with the Assembly, the extreme linearity of the Secretariat is relieved by the plasticity of the superstructure on its roof, which doubles as a kind of belvedere garden for senior bureaucrats. Pedestrian ramps, rising to the full height of the structure, angle out as narrow, incidental wings on either side of the long slab. These enclosed switchback ramps were illuminated by small apertures let into their concrete casings.

The third building, the High Court, was composed of similar tropes: It was covered by a giant concrete parasol divided into eleven vaulted bays that served to shade the entire building in conjunction with a syncopated, rhythmic *brise soleil* running across the main facade. The pattern of this concrete sunscreen indicates the presence of the eight standard courtrooms and the main tribunal, which were situated to the right and left, respectively, of the monumental entry loggia supported by three massive, largely symbolic piers rising for the full seven floors. These piers, painted green, yellow, and red, were meant to symbolize in an arcane manner the authority of the law. In his *Poème de l'Angle Droit* Le Corbusier would associate these colors with the environment, justice, and the alchemical concept of fusion, respectively. The exposed concrete access ramps lying to the rear of the court enabled Le Corbusier to establish a particularly powerful contrast between the transverse movement of the ramps and the irregular voids let into the central wall supporting them.

Perhaps the most Indian of all the monuments was the unbuilt Governor's Palace that Nehru resisted on the grounds that such a hierarchical institution was not appropriate to a democracy. The building was conceived by Le Corbusier to be the crown of the capitol complex. More than any of the other structures in the complex, the palace's composition depended upon the multilevel organization of the entire site. The building would have been approached from two different levels – from an elevated esplanade and from a sunken garden with reflecting pools, a concept taken from the traditional Mughal garden, which also had been the inspiration behind Sir Edwin Lutyen's design for the Viceroy's Palace in New Delhi. Le Corbusier's Governor's Palace was conceived as a series of superimposed platforms culminating in the upswept curve of a theatrical canopy on the roof. This was a very direct reference to the *chatris,* the characteristic parasol form of Mughal architecture.

Le Corbusier's use of his Modulor proportions in all three of these structures, and the extension of the same system to their respective positioning on the site, was a demonstration over a vast area of what the architect called "ineffable space," that is to say, a space that is infinite and beyond ultimate comprehension. The capitol was laid out on a scale in which, as architectural historian Caroline Constant has put it, Le Corbusier attempted to transcend the limits of humanist perspective so as "to achieve a new legibility that he associated with the cosmic."[12]

The human reality of the complex, and especially the urban plan of the city itself, did not always correspond to such rarefied goals. In his essay on the city, the Indian architect Charles Correa notes that "many of Le Corbusier's ideas don't work. For instance sunbreakers [*brise soleil*]: they are really great dust-catching, pigeon-infested contrivances, which gather heat all day and then radiate it back into the building at night, causing indescribable anguish to the occupants. . . . Neither have the great parasol roofs (as in the

Cross sections of the Secretariat

11.125

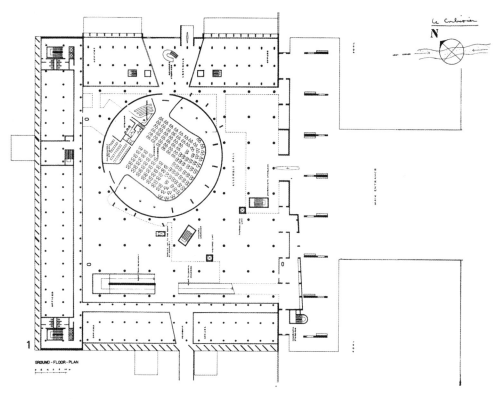

Ground-floor plan of the Assembly

Main entrance to the Secretariat

Detail of the Secretariat's monumental balcony over the main entry

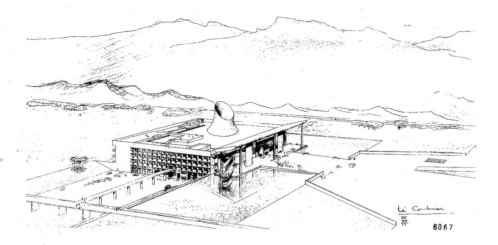

6067

Early perspective of the Assembly

Details of the Assembly's portico
with reflecting pool

11.128

High Court) proved much more useful. Was Le Corbusier perhaps more concerned with the visual expression of climate control than with its actual effectiveness?" Yet even a critic as direct as Correa must also note that the "Capitol buildings were part of [an] astonishing series of consecutive steps that make up his *oeuvre complete*." And, he notes that Nehru, the man who commissioned the new Punjabi capital, was fond of making this declaration: "It doesn't really matter whether you like Chandigarh or whether you don't like it. The fact of the matter is simply this: it has changed your lives."[13]

The focus of this cosmological invocation was a public arena in the heart of the capitol to be presided over by a monumental Open Hand pivoting in the wind, a giant sign that has, at long last, been realized. The Open Hand appears among the first sketches that Le Corbusier made during his initial visit to India in 1951. Over the years he would make the symbolic associations he attached to this form quite explicit. He characterized it as "A plastic gesture charged with a profoundly human content. A symbol very appropriate to the new situation of a liberated and independent earth. A gesture which appeals to fraternal collaboration and solidarity between all men and all nations of the world. Also a sculptural gesture . . . capable of capturing the sky and engaging the earth."[14] Elsewhere he wrote: ". . . at the moment when the Modern world gushes

forth in unlimited intellectual and material riches, one has to open the hand to receive and to give."[15] The Open Hand was the last piece to be added to the capitol; it is the symbolic key to the significance of the entire complex.

India offered to Le Corbusier not only the largest commission of his life but also the immense richness of an old and complex civilization. In his first Indian sketchbook, he wrote: "Calm, dignity, contempt for envy: perhaps India is capable of standing by them and of establishing herself at the head of civilization." Fifty years later we have to say that these high hopes have hardly been fulfilled despite the success of Chandigarh as a planned city. The capitol stands today as an indisputably heroic but ultimately sad, if not tragic, prospect. It is not only one of the great unfinished landscapes of the twentieth century but also is something of a premature ruin, currently divided by local political rivalries, which is painfully evident in the brutal partitioning of the Assembly. It also has been poorly maintained; one comes away from this heroic site with considerable nostalgia for the so-called "nonaligned" era, when it was still widely hoped that India would indeed find for itself a third way that was neither Communist nor Capitalist. Thus, at the dawn of the twenty-first century, Le Corbusier's Open Hand may still be read as the ultimate political symbol of this "third way."

11.130

A distant view of the Secretariat

A view revealing the spatial relationship between the portico of the Assembly and the Secretariat

Le Petit Cabanon

Roquebrune-Cap-Martin, France, 1951–52

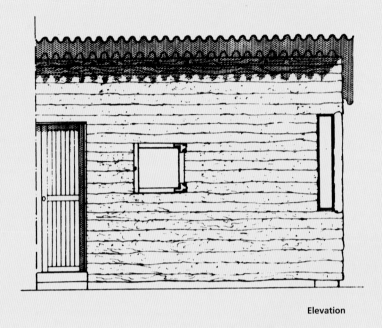

Elevation

Le Corbusier came to know the Côte d'Azur through his friendship with Jean Badovici, a Romanian émigré architect who was editor of the magazine *L'Architecture vivante.* Badovici and Eileen Gray, his intimate friend and colleague, had built a house together along the corniche of Roquebrune. This Neo-Purist seaside villa, known as E.1027, applied the principles of Le Corbusier's Five Points in a luxurious and flexible manner. After Gray gave E.1027 to Badovici in 1932, Le Corbusier and his wife, Yvonne, stayed in the house every summer as Badovici's guests. This familiarity prompted Le Corbusier to paint a number of murals in and around the house. His artistic appropriation of the villa was hardly appreciated by either Gray or Badovici, who sometime later split with Le Corbusier and forbade him to enter the house.

Despite this rupture, Le Corbusier returned to the site in the summer of 1949 with José Luis Sert, Paul Lester Weiner, and a team of draftsmen to work on their plan for Bogotá, Colombia. It was during this summer studio that he met Thomas Rebutato, the proprietor of a local restaurant situated just above E.1027. Rebutato found accommodations for the Bogotá design team, and a close relationship thereafter developed between himself and Le Corbusier. The two soon began working on several projects, including construction of five single-room rental cabins built on Rebutato's land between 1954 and 1957. In exchange for his work on this "Unité de camping," Le Corbusier received a piece of land next to Rebutato's restaurant, where in 1952 he built a vacation cabin as a present for his wife.

As the only house that Le Corbusier ever built for himself, Le Petit Cabanon is remarkable for many things, not least its size – the square shed measures just twelve feet by twelve feet in area and seven and a quarter feet in height. Inside the diminutive house, each gesture of daily life found its corresponding piece of equipment or furniture, pitched at just the right height, width, and scale. Thus, the beds, originally set at right angles to each other, had storage drawers beneath while the *colonne sanitaire,* with its stainless steel washbasin, was located in the southern corner. The toilet was screened from the entry hall by a full-height partition on which to hang coats. As architect Bruno Chiambretto has put it, "In the first sketch for the *cabanon* – a plan – not a single traditional element of architecture is represented: only pieces of furniture are indicated. At this stage of the project, they are the sole means of characterizing the space or the spaces of the *cabanon,* and only the placing of the furniture allows one to perceive the limits and the partitioning of the habitable volume. As a direct translation of the program, the furniture here constitutes the first form by which the object comes into being."[16]

The dimensions of the house and the proportions that controlled its layout exemplify Le Corbusier's Modulor system at work. The interior was organized around four interlocking rectangles each measuring 226 by 86 centimeters (7.4 by 2.8 feet) spiraling about a central square eighty-six centimeters on its sides. While the arrangement of the furniture did not always accord with this underlying

12.134

geometry, the implicit zones allocated to day and night use and the pinwheel placement of the windows corresponded to the helicoidal organization of the space. This applied particularly to the location and size of the windows, which were of Modulor dimensions and judiciously placed so that each framed a different view. Thus, a rectangular window set low over a bed afforded an inland view to the northeast while two square windows above table height had views to the southeast and southwest, respectively, with the latter capturing a panoramic view of the bay below. Each window also operated in a slightly different way. The opening to the northeast was a single-panel, side-hung window while the southeastern one consisted of two side-hung leaves. The most elaborate opening was to the southwest. It was closed by a sliding/folding double-paneled shutter lined on its inner face with a mirror so as to reflect the view when open.

Le Corbusier appears to have initially thought of the *cabanon* as an occasion to become involved once again with prefabricated, serial production. This explains why he engaged the services of Jean Prouvé and the Ajaccio builder Charles Barberis. He had invited Prouvé to work on the design of sliding windows, a system that was abandoned, along with the idea of cladding the structure in aluminum, once Prouvé withdrew from the project. In the end, the entire cabin except for its cladding was prefabricated in Ajaccio and shipped by sea and rail to Roquebrune-Cap-Martin, from whence it was manhandled to the site and assembled by Barberis under the supervision of Le Corbusier's assistant, Jacques Michel. The entire structure was framed in timber, and, except for the boarded floor and ceiling, the walls were finished in large sheets of natural plywood with thin battens covering the joints between the sheets, a technique Le Corbusier had previously employed in the Pavillon Suisse.

The last-minute decision to clad the exterior in rough, half-round logs was somewhat at odds with the precision with which the project had otherwise been conceived. Rather than being a Brutalist gesture drawn from the tectonic syntax of late Le Corbusier, it is best seen as a self-deprecating mannerism, a declaration that he would henceforth spend his vacations in a humble, Rousseauesque hut. This allusion to the primitive was reinforced in 1954 by the erection of a standard construction hut (*baraque de chantier*) on the same narrow terrace. This singular space served as his studio, or *chambre de travail,* where he wrote and painted on his vacations until his death in 1965.

Plan

1 entrance
2 door to the restaurant L' Etoile de Mer
3 closet
4 entrance to cabin
5 bathroom
6 cupboard
7 bed
8 low table
9 bed
10 "sanitary column" with washbasin
11 table
12 low shelf
13 shelf
14 vertical louvers
15 window of 28 x 28 inches
16 window of 13 x 28 inches

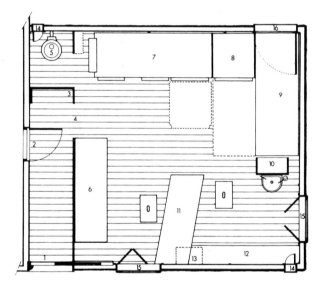

Dining table with box stools

Corner window with low table

Le Corbusier's atelier

Millowners' Association Building

Ahmedabad, India, 1951–54

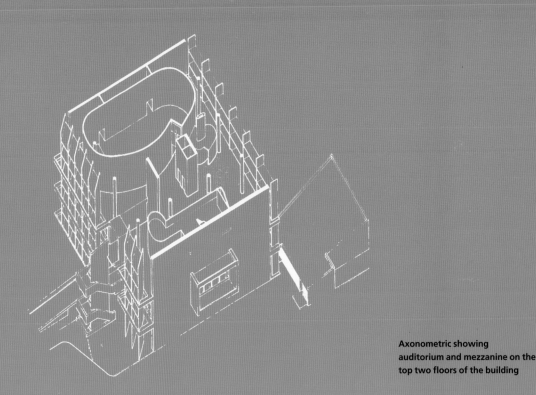

Axonometric showing
auditorium and mezzanine on the
top two floors of the building

It is an unexplainable paradox that one of the most lyrical and lucid buildings of Le Corbusier's Indian career, the Millowners' Association Building (also known as Palais des Filateurs) in Ahmedabad, has remained largely unoccupied for almost half a century. While it has been recently restored, it is now clear that it will never be used by the association for which it was originally designed.

Ahmedabad's textile industry, which experienced a "golden age" during the first half of the twentieth century, went into a seemingly irrevocable decline soon after the building was completed. But the industry's demise does not fully explain the structure's long neglect. The most plausible reason for its abandonment is that for all his concern for the essential qualities of Indian culture and climate, Le Corbusier grossly underestimated the intensity of the monsoon season. As a result, the upper part of the building was too exposed to permit its use during the rainy season. This shortcoming also was evident, to varying degrees, in his other buildings in India. In fact, one gets the impression that while Le Corbusier was very conscientious about shielding his structures from the sun and facilitating cross-ventilation, he found it difficult to adequately secure his Indian buildings against driving rain. While the lower floors of the Millowners' Association Building are fully glazed, behind their *brise soleil,* the double-height breeze hall at the top, encompassing an auditorium, is open to the elements. Clearly, this space could have been enclosed, and although some-

thing of the sort was indicated in the initial design, it was never carried through. Apart from these climatic limitations, one gets the impression that while the highly cultivated Jain industrialists were only too eager to serve as patrons, they were reluctant to give their association a cultural dimension. It is as though the structure, including its rather elaborate program, was designed to house a fictive institution. Despite this, or perhaps even because of it, the poetic power and cultural potential of the building remain indisputable.

The building is a four-story-high, eighty-nine-foot-square concrete block. Many of the primary elements of Le Corbusier's Indian work, some of which foreshadow the Carpenter Center for the Visual Arts at Harvard University, are immediately recognizable, including the building's bare concrete surfaces, its angled concrete *brise soleil,* and its rigorous, harmonic sense of proportion. One of the most powerful initial impressions of the building is its long access ramp, which slopes gently up to the main entrance foyer located at the first floor. "A ramp to the upper level," Le Corbusier explained, "made a kind of effortless smooth movement possible that affected one's perception of space in a special way ('a staircase separates . . . a ramp connects')."[17] The oval auditorium at the top level pierces the flat roof to crown the building with a concrete parasol roof. The curving profile and angular plywood sheathing of the auditorium stand in complete contrast to the calm orthogonal volume

of the containing prism. Clerestories on the eastern and western edges of the parasol allow one to look down into the auditorium from the roof garden. These apertures also admit light bouncing off the rooftop reflecting pools.

The building's carefully modulated, hierarchical program unfolds as follows: The ground floor is given over to open office space, an entry hall, and a small, single-story restaurant that sits outside the confines of the cube. The first floor, which is fed by the central external pedestrian ramp, comprises a reception area, two presidents' offices, each with its own secretarial suite, and two committee rooms. Finally, there comes the double-height breeze hall containing the hundred-seat auditorium, a bar, and a minstrel's gallery suspended on a mezzanine at the fourth-floor level. The breeze hall also is furnished in an interlocking "yin-yang" form containing male and female restrooms.

Le Corbusier reinforced the building's hierarchical organization with a consummate attention to detail. As the Indian architect Sunand Prasad has observed:

As well as stopping people from falling off and providing something to hang on to, the 'balustrade' on the left [side of the pedestrian ramp] feels safe to perch on the edge of and overhang the lawn; its wide, sloping top, which throws off rain, allows it to be relatively low, thus offering a sense of openness on the ramp. The ingeniously curved profile of the great rail on the other side makes for a 'buttock-rest' as well as an easy grip for the hand. . . . The whole composition – the solid base making special mounts for the insubstantial vertical supports, which in turn support the substantial, closely observed horizontal rail – is a poem about the heavy and the light, transparency and protection, in a new language of the materials of modern industry bound together by profoundly understood functional rigor.[18]

A similar hierarchical delicacy is to be found in the overall facing of the building. The north and south facades are rendered in brick while the floors and the walls throughout the interior are faced in Morak stone from Delhi. The syncopated vertical bands of stone – in varying widths and proportioned in accordance with the Modulor – create what Le Corbusier called a "stone tapestry."

The principle of dialogical opposition that plays a key role in so many of Le Corbusier's buildings is very evident here. The long exterior ramp to the first floor, for example, stands in strong contrast to the external dogleg stair that links the three floors of the building more intimately. The vertical, angled sun-breakers of the west facade are sharply opposed to the horizontal *brise soleil* of the eastern face. Here one would have to admit that formal considerations seem to have been paramount since the latter do little to protect against

13.144

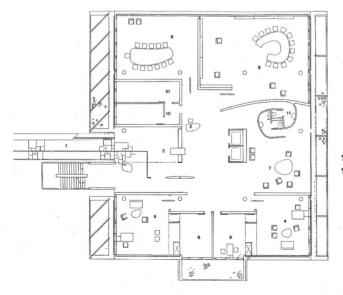

First-floor plan

1 ramp
2 entrance hall
3 information desk
4 president's office
5 vice-president's office
6 secretarial suite
7 lounge
8 committee room
9 committee room
10 general work space
11 bathrooms

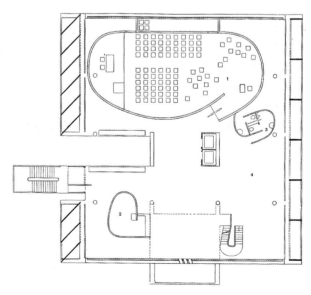

Second-floor plan

1 auditorium
2 bar and cloakroom
3 bathrooms
4 mezzanine

the early morning sun. In addition to the play of the auditorium versus the breeze hall, we also may note the dialogue between the freestanding elevator and the dogleg stair.

As Deborah Gans has observed, the Millowners' Association Building is in many respects Le Corbusier's ultimate "small palace," as he would prescribe in his 1928 essay, *"Une maison – un palais"* ("A House – A Palace"). There he attempted to demonstrate how a palace could be given all the convenience one associates with a house and how a medium-size house, through proportion, could be given the dignity of a palace. Once again, we should note that the Modulor system was used throughout in the dimensioning of the building. Evidence that the building was Le Corbusier's ultimate Indian palace includes its references to the sixteenth-century Mughal capital of India, Fatepur Sikri. This is perhaps most noticeable in the building's affinity for the open-air character of Mughal architecture. Even more telling is the way the architect envisioned the setting of the building. He wrote, "The situation of

the building in a garden dominating the river furnishes a picturesque spectacle of the cloth dyers washing and drying their cotton materials on the sand in the company of herons, cows, buffaloes and donkeys half immersed in water to keep cool. Such a panorama was an invitation to attempt, by means of the architecture, to frame views from each floor of the building for the benefit of the staff in their daily work, for festive evenings, for night views from the stage of the assembly hall, and also from the roof."[19]

This vision could hardly be further removed from the urbane culture of Paris in the 1920s, in which Le Corbusier's Purism had had its roots. This was an altogether different time and place, a moment in which, less than a decade after independence, progressive Indians would put their faith in a society based on "intermediate technology" in which both old and new, low-tech and high-tech would coexist in harmony. Thus, the cloth dyers and the cattle may be seen as the figures of an Indian miniature revitalized through the presence of an empathetic, Orientalized, architectonic modernity.

Committee room

13.148

Auditorium foyer with lavatory
cubicles in front

Stair up to the mezzanine
above the foyer

13.151

Assembly space interior

Maisons Jaoul

Paris, 1951–55

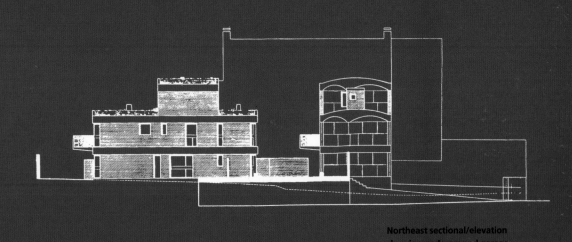

**Northeast sectional/elevation
showing underground garage**

The Maisons Jaoul, located in St. James Park in the upper-middle-class Parisian suburb Neuilly-sur-Seine, were first conceived in 1951 at the behest of André Jaoul and his wife. Jaoul had served as a client for Le Corbusier once before, commissioning a weekend house from him in 1937, two years after they first met crossing the Atlantic on the *Normandie*. Now sixteen years later, Le Corbusier's task was to design two adjoining houses – one for André Jaoul and his wife, the other for their son, Jacques Michel, and his family. Jacques Michel worked as an architect in Le Corbusier's office and would become deeply involved with the planning and construction of these twin dwellings over the next few years.

These vaulted structures, supported on load-bearing brick walls, signal the beginning of a new trend in his work; some even came to regard the Maisons Jaoul as being the first example of the so-called New Brutalist architecture. As throughout his work after 1945, the Modulor system of proportion is rigorously applied so that the houses, which are all but mirror images of each other, are both based on twin parallel bays 2.26 and 3.66 meters (7.4 and 12 feet) wide, respectively. These spans were achieved by shallow concrete vaults cast against a permanent framework of thin bricks set in place without the use of centering. These brick spans served as permanent molds for the shell concrete vaults cast in place on top of them. Tied with transverse steel rods, the vaults bear on continuous concrete beams that extend the length of each house at every floor. These beams in turn transfer the weight to load-bearing brick walls that enclose the houses on every side.

The building's syntax of exposed concrete and roughly mortared brick largely determines the "existential" character of the composition. The Maisons Jaoul's rather brutal, even solemn, texture is further emphasized by its unpainted timber fenestration, which is filled either with plate glass or insulated plywood spandrel panels. It was just this telluric, somber character that so shocked the architectural world of the time. The uneven brickwork with unstruck mortar joints, the Catalan vaults, and the rough concrete cast from boarded formwork were affronts to those who had grown up with the myth that modern architecture was invariably of frame construction, abstract, smooth-surfaced, and, above all, machinist in character. Yet the houses also served to stimulate a new generation of architects.

Set at right angles to each other, the houses impinge upon a common paved entry terrace and a subterranean garage fed by a ramp entering directly from the street. Although the two houses are similar in character, they were in fact distinctly different responses to somewhat different programs. Jacques Michel had a family to raise, and thus Maison B has three bedrooms on the first floor plus a master bedroom with bath. The house also has an east-facing roof terrace plus a studio–bedroom with a bath and terrace on the roof. Maison A, for André Jaoul, has two bedrooms plus a small chapel on the first floor and two bedrooms, each with their own shower, surrounded by terraces on the roof. Maison A has a more restricted living space at grade, capped by a double-height volume, while Maison B boasts a much larger living–dining space with

View of main stair from the living room

no double-height space. In both cases, the main two-story body of the house is capped by a bedroom pavilion while all the roofs and terraces are covered with grass, giving the whole complex a somewhat troglodyte appearance.

The houses' somber exterior tone was in marked contrast to the polychromy of the interior, particularly in Maison A, where plastered walls, cut open to allow lateral movement, have brightly colored episodes in chrome yellow and cobalt blue. These hues take on an extra radiance in the overall context of terra-cotta vaults, white tiled floors, and varnished, natural wood finishes for the cabinets and sliding partitions. A primary feature in both houses is an exposed concrete, dogleg stair cantilevered from a central concrete spine. This stair was given particular emphasis in both houses by painting the spine wall black, a tone that contrasted strongly with the concrete and with the yellow-and-white plastered walls. Similar surprising polychromatic effects extend to the exposed pipework painted in varying colors throughout both houses. In 1988, almost a quarter of a century after Le Corbusier's death, Jacques Michel would be commissioned with the task of renovating these houses.

Cross section

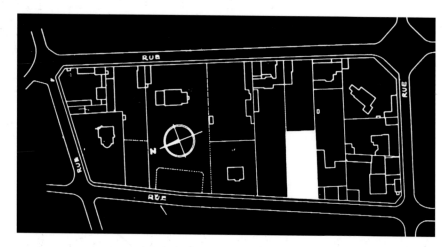

Site plan

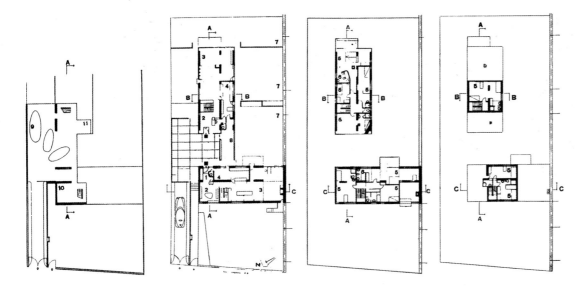

Basement, first, second, and
third floors

View from entry to sitting room

Villa Sarabhai

Ahmedabad, India, 1951–55

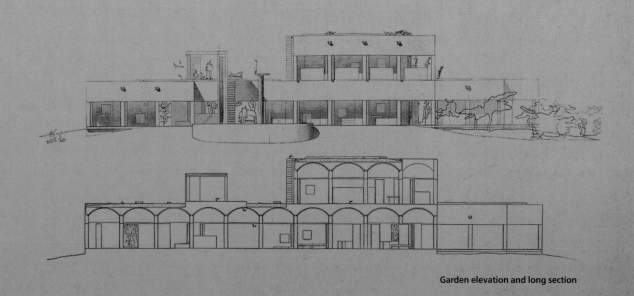

Garden elevation and long section

Le Corbusier made a general return to the vernacular around 1931, and in the decades that followed he designed a number of barrel-vaulted houses, such as the Peyrissac House in Cherchell, North Africa, in 1940, and low-rise, high-density housing settlements projected for La Sainte Baume and Roquebrune-Cap-Martin in 1949. In these works, he turned to Catalan vaulting instead of pure shell concrete construction, a hybrid device that he was to use in both the Maisons Jaoul and the Villa Sarabhai. This last, designed for Manorama Sarabhai, a wealthy widow of a textile millowner, and her son, Anand, is obviously closely linked to the Maisons Jaoul completed in Paris at virtually the same time. Both houses depart from the Neo-Purist line that was still a latent governing principle in Le Corbusier's public buildings.

Structurally speaking, the Villa Sarabhai is comprised of ten vaults set side by side. Grouped in bays of five, each of these structural counterpoints effectively divides the house into two equal parts. These sections are further subdivided into nine five-vault, one two-vault, and one three-vault volumes, articulating and accommodating distinctly different uses. The initial five-vault segment houses Mrs. Sarabhai's two-story apartment while a single-story double-vault contains the main entry and carport. To this is added a final three-vault unit comprising Anand Sarabhai's private apartment. A similarly syncopated spatial system also serves to articulate the single-story servants' quarters set to one side and in front of the main house.

As in the Maisons Jaoul, the limited spanning capacity of the brick-lined vaults is strengthened by the in situ reinforced concrete cast on the top of them. This system of construction enabled Le Corbusier to remove certain sections of the load-bearing brick structure in order to create internal space running in a contrary direction to that of the supporting beams. In this way some vestige of the free plan could be achieved without resorting to a reinforced concrete frame. In this manner Le Corbusier was able to render the Villa Sarabhai as a labyrinthine space-form. Staggered openings between the vaults allowed each apartment to unfold naturally on either side of the central entrance. At the same time continuity was sustained through the repetitive character of the brick vaults and a continuous floor surface finished in black Madrasa stone. The resultant sense of spatial displacement is enlivened still further by the alternation of roughly mortared brick walls and a number of "dematerialized" planes, wherein the brick is plastered and finished in colors ranging from white to yellow, red ocher and black, together with flashes of green. An atmosphere of Indian luxury is evoked throughout the house through such means as elevated platforms, flat wooden beds amply furnished with cushions, and even the occasional, traditional ceiling fan that, much to Le Corbusier's disapproval, came to be suspended from the crown of the vault.

Le Corbusier seems to have been particularly attentive on this occasion to reconcile his design with the rigors of the Indian climate.

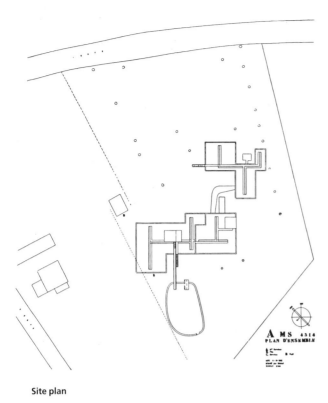

Site plan

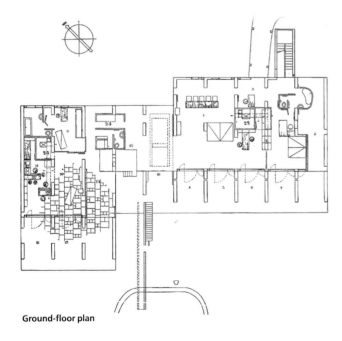

Ground-floor plan

The outriding cross-walls overlooking the garden to the southwest serve as *brise soleil* while also facilitating cross-ventilation. The elevated veranda and roof help shade the interior of the building against the intensity of the summer heat. The main veranda on the ground floor is comprised of five separate bays between brick cross-walls. Each bay serves as a kind of porch and is fitted with roller blinds to block the sun and with pivoting doors set three meters (9.8 feet) back from the end of each vault to close off the living space. These doors are fitted with mosquito screens, as are all the other openings in the house. A similar system of enclosure – veranda, *brise soleil,* and pivoting door – also prevails on the son's side of the complex.

The Villa Sarabhai presents a tranquil and modest but still imposing presence largely because of the exceptionally fertile collaboration between architect and client. Mrs. Sarabhai, for example, insisted that the Catalan vaults be closed off at their ends by concrete aprons to avoid the industrial appearance that repetitive vault ends would have created. Le Corbusier took full advantage of her felicitous demand by incorporating concrete gargoyles into the downstands on the first-floor roof terraces that discharge the heavy monsoon rains. A prominent feature of the first-floor veranda is a reinforced concrete toboggan slide/fountain that descends as a freestanding sculptural form into a rectangular paddling pool. Le Corbusier originally had designed an ovoid swimming pool, and he was disappointed that the client refused this feature on safety grounds. The sculptural and mythological unity of the work was somewhat compromised by this modification since the slide had been intended to serve as a functional link between a solitary pavilion on the roof and a pool having an equally organic shape beneath.

Despite the restrictions imposed by the cross-walls, the plan of the house has proved very adjustable over the years. It has been modified a number of times without violating the initial concept and spirit of the work. It remains in the Sarabhai family.

15.165

General view of living volume

15.166

15.168

The porter's platform in
the entry hall

Couvent Sainte-Marie de la Tourette

Eveux-sur-l'Arbresle, France, 1953–59

Cross section

If Ronchamp recalled the Hebrew Temple in the Wilderness as it had appeared in his 1923 book *Towards a New Architecture,* then the Couvent Sainte-Marie de la Tourette, near Lyons, returned Le Corbusier to one of the most synthetic experiences of his life, his visit to the Charterhouse of Ema in Tuscany, which he first saw in 1907. This monastery became the embodiment of an ideal way of life for Le Corbusier, combining, as he put it, "silence and solitude, but also daily contact with men."[20] This long-standing monastic influence on his work reached its apotheosis with the 1953 commission to provide "a home" for the Couvent Sainte-Marie de la Tourette, a new Dominican monastery at Eveux-sur-l'Arbresle. Two earlier experiences of monasteries had direct impact on his design for La Tourette – his brief stay in Mount Athos, during his so-called *Voyage d'Orient* of 1912, and a visit, late in life, to the Cistercian monastery of Le Thoronet in Provence, which had been recommended to him as an ideal model by Père Alain Couterier, who had urged him to accept the commission for the Chapel of Nôtre Dame-du Haut in Ronchamp despite the fact that he belonged to a different denomination.

The steeply sloping site at Eveux gave Le Corbusier little choice but to divide the sectional organization of the building between a pedestrian entry on the upper part of the site and vehicular access to the kitchens and parking set some ten meters (thirty-three feet) below. Thus, the building presents itself at two different scales depending on whether one approaches from the high ground,

through the woods, by passing the main entrance of the old château, or if one comes from the valley below, where the monumental five-story mass rises like a cliff (a reference to Mount Athos) before a rolling greensward sweeping down from the building into the distant woods. In this way the monastery enters into an extremely dichotomous interplay with its site, of which Colin Rowe wrote in 1961, "Architecture and landscape, lucid and separate experiences, are like the rival protagonists of a debate who progressively contradict and clarify each other's meaning."[21]

La Tourette gave the monastic paradigm a somewhat secular cast by replacing the traditional unifying cloister with a more efficient, centralized system of distribution. This assumed the form of a suspended, T-shaped ambulatory that connected the monastery's main staircases, which were situated at the midpoint of three sides of the rectangular court around which the building was structured. This wide passageway, connecting the chapel on the north with the refectory on the west and classrooms on the south, also accessed two tiers of monks' cells stacked on top of one another around three sides of the central court. This cloister was given a syncopated visual rhythm by virtue of its floor-to-ceiling glass panes of varying width held in place by concrete mullions. This curtain wall, to which Le Corbusier gave the name of *pan de verres ondulatiores,* also was applied to one side of the monastery's public spaces. One gets the impression that this varying vertical rhythm was meant to express the movement of the monks as they pursued

16.172

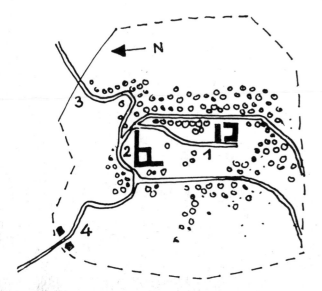

View from the southwest

Site plan
1 new monastery
2 former house of the
Dominican fathers

their daily rounds. In addition to this cloister, the monastery also is served by two other, more intimate circulation systems. A continuous corridor connects the oratory, the common rooms, the classrooms, and the library to the main entry while a gallery running around the inner perimeter of the central court on two floors affords access to the monks' cells. These two corridors are lit by narrow clerestories while the teaching spaces below are faced with thin concrete panels interspersed with glass panes in a counterchanging swastika formation.

The monks' cells, which measure 1.83 or 2.26 meters (6 or 7.4 feet) wide, depending on the status of the resident, are provided with private concrete balconies. Cross-ventilation is induced in the cells and elsewhere by pivoting, full-height louvers covered with mosquito screens. These *"aérateurs"* are fabricated out of light metal or wood depending on their location and height. The public spaces are ventilated by larger versions of the same device.

While the chapel is treated as a virtually windowless volume, its reinforced concrete form is nonetheless discretely lit by vertical, full-height openings of varying width and by narrow, partially concealed clerestories running along either side of the nave. These last provide an alternating pattern of colored light, permutations of red, yellow, and green along the nave's northern and southern faces. Direct sunlight enters this space in a more dramatic fashion at certain times of the day, particularly at sunset, when the flat roof of the chapel appears to detach itself from the dark, enclosing walls on which it rests, particularly when a shaft of golden light penetrates just below the soffit of the ceiling.

The vestry and the crypt, to the south and north of the chapel, respectively, are treated as subterranean worlds, lit from above by two different types of *"canons à lumière"* angled so as to receive zenithal light at different times during the day. Revealed on the exterior as a bulbous concrete mass bursting out of the chapel's northern flank, the crypt is reached by a sequestered stairway and corridor that pass beneath the nave; then the corridor opens up to a stepped ramp giving access to the crypt's seven altars. The Piranesian drama of this space is partly due to the fact that its bounding concrete walls cant inward to varying degrees as they rise upward. The entire volume is activated by a subtle color treatment that changes according to one's position in the space and to the time of day. The solid concrete wall separating the crypt from the church is painted red,

black, and yellow on different parts of its surface while large ovoid top-lights, colored red and white, are set into the flat concrete ceiling covering the space. This ceiling's pale blue hue seems to change according to the ambient light and the position of the spectator.

More of a citadel than a monastery, La Tourette lies suspended above its site in a somewhat ambiguous fashion. While the inaccessible interior courtyard remains open to the sky and the roofs on the T-shaped ambulatory are covered in grass, there are extensive areas of bare ground beneath the building that never receive any sun. This leftover space is rendered all the more unusable by multiple concrete piers that support the structure above. Thus, at La Tourette, as in buildings throughout Le Corbusier's career, the unresolved space beneath the *pilotis* compromises a work that otherwise demonstrates the full scope of his exceptional talent.

La Tourette has continued to serve its monastic function with only a few changes over the years. Some of these changes have been due to a change in Catholic policy with regard to the way monks should live and be trained in a modern, secular age. While there are very few monks in residence today, La Tourette continues to function as an important center for the Dominicans while at the same time serving as a public conference center.

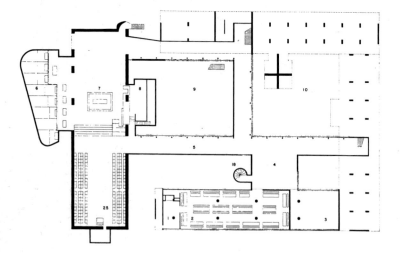

16.174

Second-floor plan

1 pantry
2 refectory
3 chapter house
4 atrium
5 main corridor
6 crypt altars
7 high altar
8 vestry
9, 10 open court
18 stair to court
25 chapel

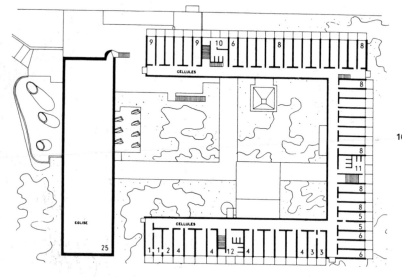

Fifth-floor plan

1 sick-bay
2 surgery
3 guest cells
4 instructors
5 master of novices
6 novices' cells
8 lay brothers
10, 11 bathrooms
25 chapel

View of the *canons a' lumiere* penetrating the roof of the side chapel

Typical access corridor

Interior of the chapel at the point
of the altar and crossing

Carpenter Center for the Visual Arts

Harvard University, Cambridge, Massachusetts, 1961–64

Section through transversal pedestrian ramp

Finished in 1964, a year before his death at age 78, the Carpenter Center for the Visual Arts is the only building Le Corbusier realized in the United States. It is a *tour de force* in more ways than one since the architect was aware that this was surely his last chance to realize a built manifesto in North America. This accounts for the way in which he incorporated the full gamut of his architectural repertoire within the confines of a relatively small building. At the same time the building acquired its own idiosyncratic form from the constraints of its extremely tight and demanding site. Thus, the building deliberately opposes the character of its context, the dense traditional fabric of Harvard University. Rather than harmonize with the Neo-Georgian structures to either side – the Fogg Art Museum and the Faculty Club – and instead of conforming to the orthogonal grain of Harvard Yard just across the street, Le Corbusier created a pinwheeling figure, set on a diagonal, as a foil with which to heighten through its spatial turbulence the rather traditional character of adjacent frontages. He began with the idea of a spiral but soon transformed this into a pedestrian ramp that crossed diagonally from front to back through the mid-point of the building.

Le Corbusier was able to graft onto this schismatic figure two elliptical appendages dilating to either side of the ramp and turning forward and backward toward the streets. These outriding wings, elevated on *pilotis,* bulge out from the central half-cube of the building to accommodate art studios on the first and second floors. The rest of the program consolidates about this figure. A reception and conference room – which now serves as additional gallery space – are housed in the slightly recessed ground floor with the director's office and the first-floor studio immediately above. The pedestrian ramp enters the building at the second floor with a second studio lying to one side and a partially double-height exhibition hall opening up on the other. All these levels are served by a central vertical elevator and stair core. The building is crowned by a penthouse for the resident artist.

Except for the floor-to-ceiling glass brick panels of the vertical core, the building fabric is of reinforced concrete throughout. Rather than the classic, boarded formwork used in other projects such as the Unité d'Habitation in Marseilles – which imparts a characteristic wood grain to the material – the concrete was cast on site using steel sheet molds or plastic-coated plywood, thereby guaranteeing a smooth finish. Frameless plate glass was set directly into the concrete and shielded by fixed concrete *brise soleil,* angled according to the exposure.

The continuous vertical fenestration of the studios, interposed with concrete mullions, is occasionally interrupted by Le Corbusier's patented *aerateurs* – narrow floor-to-ceiling ventilating panels, which are similar to those used in La Tourette and in the Secretariat

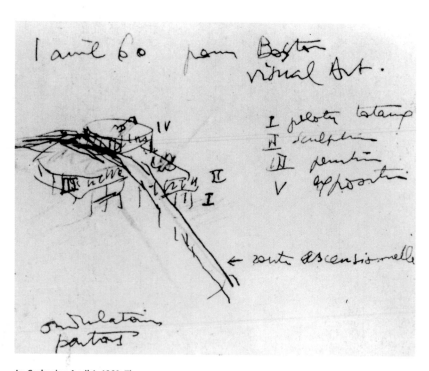

17.184

Le Corbusier. April 1, 1960. The
partly-illegible key in Roman
numerals reads: I. *pilotis* II. Sculpture
III. Painting V. exhibition

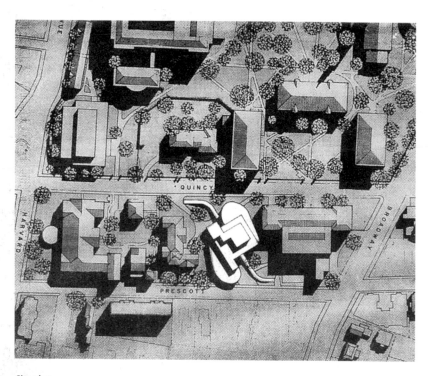

Site plan

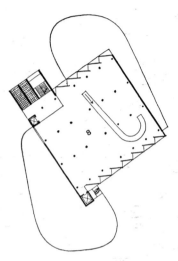

Second-floor plan

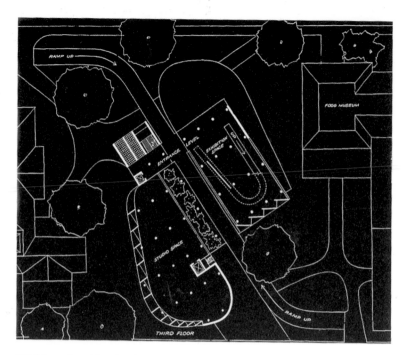

Third-floor plan with pedestrian
ramp passing through it

Detail of the glass-block wall
of the main stair

in Chandigarh. These manually operated vents were fully capable
of providing air circulation when needed and served as a kind of
protest against the American fixation on air-conditioning. Of this
profligate use of energy Le Corbusier wrote, "Air conditioning,
dear to Americans with their by now traditional sinuses, will certainly be able to function during cold periods, but I think that the
spaces can be ventilated with fresh air from the outside without
mechanical exchange, when spring shines on the exterior. Air-
conditioning can intervene again in the hot periods (if you sirs
are not found completely naked on Cape Cod)."[22] Be this as it may,
the intolerance of the client for the humidity that accompanies
the long, hot summers of the East Coast eventually led to full air-
conditioning being installed throughout.

Pedestrian ramp exiting
from the building on the north-
western side

Interior of one of the main
studios showing *ondulatoire*
fenestration

Zenithal light in the corner of a
studio space

**Eastern front opening onto
Prescott Street**

Western facade

Chronology of Realized Buildings

The dates provided below, obtained from
Fondation Le Corbusier in Paris, represent the year
of each project's commencement.

Year	Building	Location
1905	Villa Fallet	La Chaux-de-Fonds, Switzerland
1907	Villa Stotzer	La Chaux-de-Fonds
1907	Villa Jacquemet	La Chaux-de-Fonds
1912	Villa Favre-Jacot	Le Locle, Switzerland
1912	Villa Jeanneret	La Chaux-de-Fonds
1916	Villa Schwob	La Chaux-de-Fonds
1916	Cinema "La Scala"	La Chaux-de-Fonds
1917	Chateau d'Eau	Bordeaux, France
1917	Cite Ouvriere	Saint Nicholas d'Aliermont, France
1921	Amenagement de la Villa Berque	Paris
1922	Villa Besnus	Vaucresson, France
1922	Maison-Atelier Ozenfant	Paris
1923	Villas La Roche-Jeanneret	Paris
1923	La Petite Maison, a.k.a. Villa "Le Lac"	Corseaux, Switzerland
1923	Villa Lipchitz-Miestchaninoff	Boulogne, France
1923	Villa Ternisien	Boulogne
1924	Lotissement de Lege	Bordeaux
1924	Maison du Tonkin	Bordeaux
1924	Quartiers Modernes Fruges	Bordeaux
1924	Pavillon de l'Esprit Nouveau	Paris
1924	Villa Planeix	Paris
1926	Armée du Salut, Palais du Peuple	Paris
1926	Maison Cook	Boulogne, France
1926	Maison Guiette	Antwerp, Belgium
1926	Villa Stein de Monzie	Vaucresson
1927	Villas Weissenhof-Siedlung	Stuttgart, Germany
1927	Pavillon Nestlé	Paris
1927	Villa Church	Ville d'Avray, France
1928	Villa Baizeau	Carthage, Tunisia
1928	Centrosoyus	Moscow, Russia
1928	Villa Savoye	Poissy, France
1929	Cité de Refuge	Paris
1929	Armée du Salut, Asile Flottant	Paris
1929	Appartment de Beistegui	Paris
1929	Villa de Mandrot	Le Pradet, France
1930	Immeuble Clarté	Geneva, Switzerland
1930	Pavillon Suisse, Cité Universitaire	Paris
1931	Immeuble Porte Molitor – Appartement Le Corbusier	Paris
1934	Maison de Weekend	La Celle Saint Cloud, France
1935	Villa Le Sextant	Les Mathes, France
1936	National Ministry of Education	Rio de Janeiro, Brazil
1936	Pavillon des Temps Nouveaux	Paris
1938	Centre de Readaptation des Jeunes Chomeurs	Paris
1945	Unité d'Habitation de Marseilles	Marseilles, France
1946	Usine Duval	Saint Die, France
1949	Villa du Docteur Curutchet	Buenos Aires, Argentina
1950	Chapel of Nôtre Dame-du-Haut	Ronchamp, France
1950	Chandigarh, Capital of the Punjab	Chandigarh, India
1951	Le Petit Cabanon	Roquebrune-Cap-Martin, France
1951	Millowners' Association Building	Ahmedabad, India
1951	Maisons Jaoul	Paris
1951	Villa Sarabhai	Ahmedabad
1951	Villa Shodan	Ahmedabad
1951	Museum	Ahmedabad
1952	Unité d'Habitation de Reze	Reze, France
1952	Haute Cour	Chandigarh
1952	Museum and Art Gallery	Chandigarh
1953	Secretariat	Chandigarh
1953	Club Nautique	Chandigarh
1953	Couvent Sainte-Marie de la Tourette	Eveux-sur-l'Arbresle, France
1953	Maison du Brazil, Cite Universitaire	Paris
1955	Tombe Le Corbusier	Roquebrune-Cap-Martin
1955	Assembly	Chandigarh
1955	Barrage	Bhakra, India
1956	Stade	Firminy, France
1956	Stade	Baghdad, Iraq
1956	Unité d'Habitation de Briey en Foret	Briey-en-Foret, France
1956	Maison de la Culture	Firminy
1957	Unité d'Habitation de Berlin	Berlin, Germany
1957	Musee d'Art Occidental	Tokyo, Japan
1958	Pavillon Philips	Brussels, Belgium
1959	Ecole d'Art	Chandigarh
1960	Unité d'Habitation de Firminy	Firminy
1960	Ecluse de Kembs Niffer	Kembs, France
1961	Carpenter Center for the Visual Arts, Harvard University	Cambridge, Massachusetts
1963	Centre Le Corbusier, Heidi Weber	Zurich, Switzerland

Acknowledgments

In addition to the indispensable scholarly entries that make up the remarkably comprehensive and detailed compendium *Le Corbusier, une encyclopédie* of 1987, I would like to acknowledge certain historians, architects, and critics who have contributed to my knowledge of the work of this singular figure, among them Tim Benton, H. Allen Brooks, Caroline Constant, Alan Colquhoun, Charles Correa, William Curtis, Norma Evenson, Mogens Kustrup, Mary McLeod, Stanislaus von Moos, José Oubrerie, Danièle Pauly, Colin Rowe, Bruno Reichlin, Arthur Ruegg, Edward Sekler, Patricia Sekler, Brian Brace Taylor, Adolf Max Vogt, and Ivan Zaknic. As the footnotes and the selected bibliography indicate, in the case of this monographic treatment I am particularly indebted to the writings of Jacques Sbriglio, chiefly his three studies produced for the Fondation Le Corbusier (1996–1999); respectively, *Apartment Block 24 N.C. & Le Corbusier's Home, The Villas La Roche-Jeanneret,* and *The Villa Savoye.*

Furthermore, I am most indebted to Bruno Chiambretto for his study *Le Corbusier à Cap-Martin* (1987). Specific to Le Corbusier's work in India, I have had recourse to the occasional writings of Charles Correa, Kiran Joshi, and Sunand Prasad. Finally, I have to acknowledge a major debt to Deborah Gans' beautifully written and exhaustively researched *The Le Corbusier Guide* (1987). Beyond this there lie those who have contributed in more productive and artistic ways, my assistant Amanda Johnson, my editors Diana Murphy and Richard Olsen, the graphic designer Judy Hudson of Biproduct, and above all, given the nature of this book, the photographer Roberto Schezen.

Kenneth Frampton
New York City, 2002

Notes

1   R. H. L. Herbert, ed., *Modern Artists on Art* (Englewood Cliffs, New Jersey: Prentice Hall, 1964), 73.

2   Le Corbusier, *Towards a New Architecture* (London, England: Rodker, 1931), 1.

3   See the special commemorative issue of *Aujourd'hui, Art et Architecture* 51 (November 1965): 10.

4   Colin Rowe, "The Mathematics of the Ideal Villa," *The Mathematics of the Ideal Villa and Other Essays* (Cambridge, Mass.: MIT Press, 1976), 1–17.

5   W. Boesiger, ed., *Le Corbusier: Complete Works 1910–1929, Volume II*, 6th ed. (Zurich, Switzerland: Birkhauser, 1996), 186.

6   Jacques Sbriglio, *Le Corbusier: The Villa Savoye* (Paris, France and Basel, Switzerland: Fondation Le Corbusier/Birkhauser, 1999), 97.

7   Brian Brace Taylor, *Le Corbusier: The City of Refuge, Paris 1929–33* (Chicago, Illinois: The University of Chicago Press, 1987), 20.

8   Just prior to World War II Le Corbusier was working on a type of prefabricated, all metal, lightweight, two-story housing type to be assembled dry, his so-called M.A.S. houses. See W. Boesiger, ed., *Le Corbusier: Complete Works 1938–1946, Volume IV* (Zurich, Switzerland: Birkhauser, 1996), 38–41.

9   Deborah Gans, *The Le Corbusier Guide* (New York: Princeton Architectural Press, 1987), 39.

10 For a detailed analysis of the iconography of this mural, see Richard Moore, *Le Corbusier: Images and Symbols* (Atlanta, Georgia: Georgia State University Press, 1977). See also Richard Moore, "Alchemical and Mythical Themes in the Poem of the Right Angle 1947–1965," *Oppositions* 19–20 (Cambridge, Mass.: MIT Press, 1980): 110–139. See also Mogens Krustrup, *Porte Email* (Copenhagen, Denmark: Architektens Forlag, 1991), 28–31.

11 See Danièle Pauly, *Le Corbusier: The Chapel at Ronchamp* (Paris, France, and Basel, Switzerland: Fondation Le Corbusier/Birkhauser, 1997), 59.

12 Caroline Constant, "From the Virgilian Dream to Chandigarh: Le Corbusier and the Modern Landscape," *Denatured Visions: Landscape and Culture in the Twentieth Century* (New York: The Museum of Modern Art, 1991), 86.

13 Charles Correa, "Chandigarh: The View from Benares," *Architecture + Design*, 3(6) (September-October 1987): 73–75.

14 See Mary Patricia May Sekler, "Ruskin, the Tree and the Open Hand," *The Open Hand: Essays on Le Corbusier* (Cambridge, Mass.: MIT Press, 1977), 75.

15 Le Corbusier, *Creation is a Patient Search* (New York: Praeger, 1960), 278.

16 Bruno Chiambretto, *Le Corbusier à Cap-Martin* (Marseilles, France: Éditions Parenthèses, 1987), 38.

17 W. Boesiger, ed., *Le Corbusier: Complete Works 1952–1957* (Zurich, Switzerland: Birkhauser, 1996), 144.

18 Sunand Prasad, "Le Corbusier in India," *Le Corbusier, Architect of the Century* (London, England: Arts Council of Great Britain, 1987), 300.

19 W. Boesiger, ed., *Le Corbusier: Complete Works 1952–1957* (Zurich, Switzerland: Birkhauser, 1996), 146.

20 Jean Petit, *Le Corbusier: Lui-même* (Geneva, Switzerland: Éditions Rousseau, 1970), 28.

21 Colin Rowe, "La Tourette," *The Mathematics of the Ideal Villa and Other Essays* (Cambridge, Mass.: MIT Press, 1977), 188.

22 Edward F. Sekler and William Curtis, *Le Corbusier at Work: The Genesis of the Carpenter Center for Visual Arts* (Cambridge, Mass.: Harvard University Press, 1978), 169.

Selected Bibliography

Becket, D. "A Study of Le Corbusier's Poème de l'Angle Droit." MPhil thesis, Cambridge University, 1980

Benton, Tim. *The Villas of Le Corbusier 1920–1930*. New Haven, Conn.: Yale University Press, 1987

Besset, Maurice. *Oui est Le Corbusier?* Geneva, Switzerland: Skira, 1968

Bloc, A., P. Lacombe, and P. Goulet, eds. Commemorative issue of *Aujourd'hui, Art et Architecture,* no. 51, November 1965

Brooks, H. Allen, ed. *Le Corbusier's Formative Years*. Chicago: University of Chicago Press, 1997

———, ed. *Le Corbusier*. New York: Princeton Architectural Press, 1987

Chiambretto, Bruno. *Le Corbusier à Cap-Martin*. Paris, France: Éditions Parenthèses, 1987

Cohen, Jean-Louis. *Le Corbusier and the Mystique of the USSR: Theories and Projects for Moscow, 1928–1936*. New York: Princeton Architectural Press, 1992

Colquhoun, A. "Formal and Functional Interactions: A Study of Two Late Works by Le Corbusier," *Essays in Architectural Criticism: Modern Architecture and Historical Change*. Cambridge, Mass.: MIT Press, 1985

Constant, Caroline. "From the Virgilian Dream to Chandigarh; Le Corbusier and the Modern Landscape," *Denatured Visions: Landscape and Culture in the Twentieth Century*. Stuart Wrede and William H. Adams. New York: Harry N. Abrams, 1991

Curtis, William J.R. *Le Corbusier: Ideas and Forms*. London: Phaidon Press, 1986

Evenson, Norma. *Chandigarh*. Berkeley: University of California Press, 1966

———. *The Machine and the Grand Design*. New York: Studio Vista, 1969

Gans, Deborah. *The Le Corbusier Guide*. New York: Princeton Architectural Press, 1987

Gresleri, Giuliano. *Il Viaggio in Toscana*. Venice, Italy: Marsilio, 1987

———and Italo Zannier. *Le Corbusier Viaggio in Oriente*, Gli inediti di Charles Edouard Jeanneret, fotografe e scrittore (Fondation Le Corbusier, Paris). Venice, Italy: Marsilio, 1984

Gubler, Jacques. "In Time with the Swiss Watchmakers," *Le Corbusier: Early Works by Charles-Édouard Jeanneret-Gris*. New York: St. Martin's Press, 1987

Harris, Elizabeth Davis. *Le Corbusier, Riscos Brasileiros*. São Paulo: Nobel, 1987

Henze, Anton. *La Tourette: The Le Corbusier Monastery*. New York: George Wittenborn, 1966

Lapunzina, Alejandro. *Le Corbusier's Maison Curutchet*. New York: Princeton Architectural Press, 1997.

Le Corbusier. *Aircraft*. London: The Studio, 1987; reprint Paris: Trefail/Adam Biro, 1987

———. *Almanach d'architecture moderne*. Paris: Éditions Crès et Cie, 1925

———. *L'Art décoratif d'aujord'hui*. Paris: Éditions Crès et Cie, 1925

———. *La Charte d'Athènes*. Paris: Plon, 1943

———. *L'Espirit Nouveau*, nos. 1–28. 1920–25

———. *Une Maison, un palais*. Paris: Éditions Crès et Cie, 1928

———. *Manière de penser l'urbanisme*. Paris: L'Architecture d'aujourd'hui, 1946

———. *Mise au point*. Paris: Force-Vivres, 1966

———. *Le Modulor*. Boulogne, France: L'Architecture d'aujourd'hui, 1950

———. *Le Modulor 2: la parole est aux usagers*. Paris: L'Architecture d'aujourd'hui, 1955

———. *Le Poème de l'angle droit*. Paris: Tériade, 1955

———. *Précisions sur l'état présent de l'architecture et de l'urbanisme*. Paris: Éditions Crès et Cie, 1930

———. *Quand les cathedrals étaient blanches*. Paris: Plon, 1937

———. *Les Trois Établissements humains*. Paris: Denoël, 1945

———. *Urbanisme*. Paris: Éditions Crès et Cie, 1925

———. *Vers une architecture*. Paris: Éditions Crès et Cie, 1923

———. *La Ville Radieuse*. Boulogne, France: L'Architecture d'aujourd'hui, 1935

———. *Voyage d'Orient*. Carnets 1–6. Milan, Italy: Electa Le Moniteur, 1987

Lucan, Jacques, ed. *Le Corbusier: une encyclopédie*. Paris: Editions du Centre Pompidou, 1987

McLeod, M. "Le Corbusier and Algiers," *Oppositions*, 19–20, Winter–Spring 1980

———. "Architecture or Revolution: Taylorism, Technocracy, and Social Change," *Art Journal*, Summer 1983: 132–47

———. "Urbanism and Utopia, Le Corbusier from Regionalism to Vichy," PhD thesis, Princeton University, 1985

Maier, C.S. "Between Taylorism and Technocracy: European Ideologies and the Vision of Industrial Productivity in the 1920s," *Journal of Contemporary History*, 5, 1970: 27–61

Moore, R. "Alchemical and Mythical Themes in the Poem of the Right Angle, 1945–65," *Oppositions*, 19–20, Winter-Spring 1980: 111–39

Pauly, Danièle. *Le Corbusier: La Chapelle de Ronchamp*. Basel, Switzerland: Birkhäuser Verlag, 1997

Petit, Jean. *Le Corbusier: Lui-même*. Geneva, Switzerland: Editions Rousseau, 1970

Sbriglio, Jacques. *Le Corbusier: L'Unité d'habitation de Marseille*. Marseilles, France: Éditions Parenthèses, 1992

Sekler, E.F. and W. Curtis. *Le Corbusier at Work: The Genesis of the Carpenter Center For the Visual Arts*. Cambridge, Mass.: Harvard University Press, 1978

Serenyi, Peter. "Le Corbusier, Fourier and the Monastery of Ema," *Art Bulletin*, XLIX, 1967, 277–86; reprinted in Serenyi, ed., *Le Corbusier in Perspective*. Englewood Cliffs, New Jersey: Prentice Hall, 1975

Taylor, Brian Brace. *Le Corbusier: The City of Refuge, Paris 1929–1933*. Paris, France: Équerre, 1980

Treib, Marc. *Space Calculated in Seconds*. Princeton: Princeton University Press, 1996

Turner, Paul V. *The Education of Le Corbusier*. Cambridge, Mass.: Harvard University Press, 1971

Vogt, Adolf Max. *Le Corbusier, the Noble Savage: Toward an Archaeology of Modernism*. Cambridge, Mass.: MIT Press, 1998

Walden, Russell, ed., *The Open Hand: Essays on Le Corbusier*. Cambridge, Mass.: MIT Press, 1977

Zaknic, Ivan. *The Final Testament of Père Corbu*. New Haven, Conn.: Yale University Press, 1997

Archives:

Le Courbusier Sketchbooks. In 4 volumes. Edited by Andre Wogenscky and Francois de Franclieu. Cambridge, Mass.: MIT press, 1973

Œuvres completes, 1910–1965. In 8 volumes. Edited by Willy Boesiger. Zurich: Girsberger, 1930–1971; reprinted as 8-volume boxed set in Boesiger, ed., *Le Corbusier: Complete Works*. Basel, Switzerland: Birkhäuser Verlag, 1996.

The Le Corbusier Archive. In 32 volumes. Edited by Allen H. Brooks. New York: Garland Publishing Company/ Fondation Le Corbusier, 1982–1984

Index

Italized page numbers refer to illustrations.

Credits